To my parents, Aron and Riva Gankin,
to whom I owe everything.

To my husband, Boris Mordukhovich,
who shares my life for more than fifty years.

To my beautiful daughters, Lena and Irina,
who are the joy and pride of my life.

To my beloved grandchildren, Becky, Polly, Mia,
Aron, Yael, and Natan, who will continue passing
the light from generation to generation.

Table Of Contents

PART 1
Childhood, Family, Roots

My First Life

MARGARET
MORDUKHOVICH

SPARK Publications
Charlotte, North Carolina

MY FIRST LIFE
Margaret Mordukhovich

Designed, produced, and published by
SPARK Publications
SPARKpublications.com
Charlotte, North Carolina

Digital imaging by SPARK Publications.
Photos supplied by the Author's family.
Additional graphics: h.yegho, pics five, sociologas / shutterstock.com

Printed in the United States of America

Paperback, September 2024, ISBN: 978-1-953555-73-1

Library of Congress Control Number: 2024918844

PART 2
Between Two Lives

PART 1

Childhood, Family, Roots

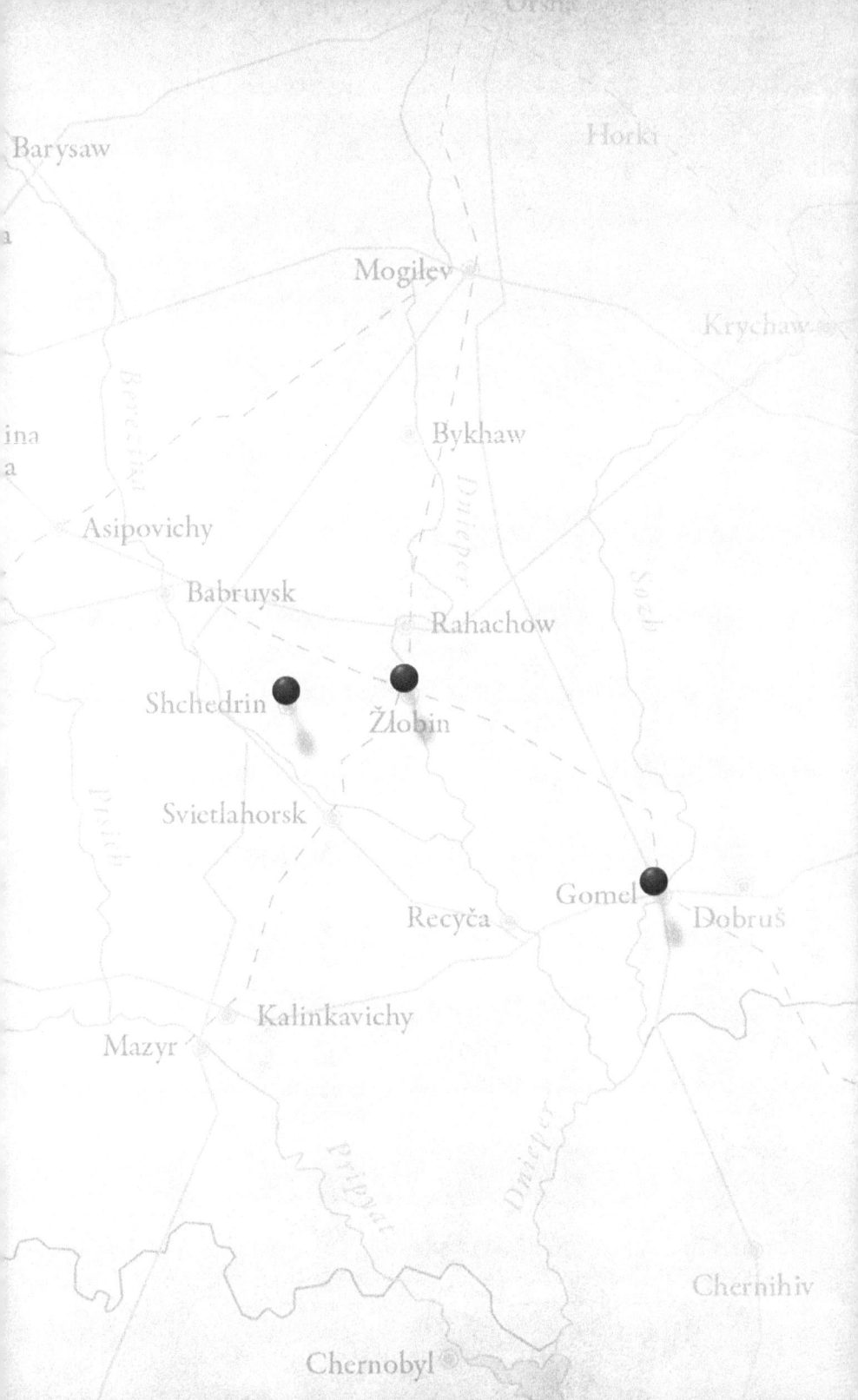

CHAPTER 1

Introduction

My favorite photo

I am looking at this picture of a little girl with an abundance of curly hair. Who is she? Why is she so serious? I see the unsmiling face of a child, big eyes, gray dress. I remember this dress very well—the slightly crooked stitches, the red collar. Why do I remember it so vividly, even now, many years later? Is it because I owned so few dresses? Is it because my mom sewed it by hand? Of course, but then again, she sewed everything by hand. She had no sewing machine. This was the postwar Soviet Union, our tiny room, and my parents, my lucky parents who had lost everything in the war. Their first house, their modest furniture, their white linens—all of it became black smoke, all but themselves. They survived. Their lives were forever divided by the most heinous war of the twentieth century, just as mine would be divided by immigration—the before and the after.

Before that war, there was early childhood, school, siblings, revolution, hunger, World War I, German occupation, civil war, no rights, no religious freedom—a normal life for two children born in Russia in 1912. They both came from long lines of rabbis. What could have been worse than that in the twenties and thirties in the Soviet Union?

Wikipedia has an article titled "Lishenets," which means that this word is now known in English-speaking countries. The term describes people who were officially disenfranchised in the Soviet Union for eighteen long years, from 1918 to 1936. Private merchants, clergy, manufacturers, successful farmers, and many other categories of people were on this list. These people were not just denied the right to vote; this status affected most aspects of their and their children's lives. One of the striking examples— they and their children were not allowed to receive higher or technical education.

All of this definitely impacted the fate of my parents. My mom wanted to be a medical doctor. She went far away to Stalingrad, where nobody knew that she was the daughter of a rabbi. She was admitted to the medical college but contracted typhus, barely survived it, then relapsed and barely survived it again. Being very weak, she had to quit school and go back to Gomel to be with her parents. Mom would have made a fine doctor, I am sure; she was very kind, very perceptive, and very smart. Instead, she became a bookkeeper. Dad was able to enter university only in 1936, at twenty four, when the government finally lifted all the restrictions.

Aron and Riva Gankin

I am sure they tried to conform; children always do. They worked, studied, sang Soviet songs, and wore Soviet clothes. They were young; they met, fell in love, and married in 1935. In a year, their son was born. He was named after my mom's grandfather Rabbi Boruch Komissarov. His Hebrew name was Boruch, but no one knew about it. Officially, he was Boris, just a regular Boris, like the son of their Russian neighbor. He was circumcised, but God forbid the neighbors find out. People were arrested left and right for "lesser" offenses. There must have been something those people did wrong—a skipped meeting, an incautious joke, a reckless word. Be careful; the walls have ears; your tongue is your enemy; lower your voice.

Normal life, happy life—let it stay like this. Three more months of savings, and they will be able to buy a kitchen table to replace the one my mom built by herself. No, she didn't need a new dress; look how nicely she darned the old one. No one will ever notice. She would rather buy a new suit for her husband.

Then the war began. The curly-haired girl was not born yet—in fact, she would be born many years later—but her mother was a natural storyteller, and the girl was very affected by all of Mom's stories. She knew all about it! She could almost see the fires and smell the smoke. No one tried to scare her, to traumatize the poor baby. She was born into love. She was never hungry, even when her mom was.

With Mom

Look at another picture. Here, the girl is almost one year old. Her mom is holding her in her arms—a skinny mom holding her chubby baby. The baby's face is wider than the tired face of this woman. Mom is happy. The war is over. Her husband came back. Her son survived. So many children died during the war from disease, from hunger, from bombardments. She feels so lucky. She saved her son and her father, her husband was home with her, and now her daughter was born. She is so happy and she smiles. She is thirty-seven. She has lost all her natural teeth to wartime scurvy. She smiles with her new metal teeth. She is content. It is summer, and probably hot. Small beads of sweat cover her face.

"Mom, in this picture, why are you in this warm dress?"

"Hah, hah, this was the only dress I had then. You will never guess what I made it from. It's from your dad's old trench coat. I made it myself—a needle, a thread, and my bare fingers. I used to wash it in the evening and then iron it for an hour to dry. Your dress? What about it? No, it's not made from your dad's trench coat. It is from his old pants. Look—this is good material, wool, prewar, and the collar is from your brother's tie. Smart, isn't it? You are the best-dressed girl in our apartment building, and the prettiest. You will grow up to be a beauty. You'll be smart and tall and never know any war."

Why is this girl so serious? Why do I always look so serious, almost sad? Was I scared of my mom's stories? What are this girl's first memories? What are my earliest memories? Can my words bring this girl back? Can they bring back my mom, full of energy? Bring back her sparkling eyes, her jokes, her dedication, her unconditional love for my dad, for all of us? Can they bring back my shy, gentle dad? Can I remember only the things I prefer to remember? Can I skip whole chapters? Can I close the door when I want it to stay closed? Can I write not about me, but about this little girl?

Little girl, why are you so serious? Look at me. I know several things about you, things that really matter. Give me your little hand. I am not a palm reader, but I know your future, at least to a certain point. You will almost die at ten, but you will survive. You will grow up. You will read a lot, write poems, date. You will marry and have kids. Oh yes, you will have children; this is very important. You will work all your life. Actually, you will have not one but two lives: before and after immigration.

Look at me, little girl, whose first language and first culture were Russian, who knew nothing about religion, but everything about Jewishness. How old were you when you began to understand love and hatred, fear and courage, grief and happiness, war and peace? Why do you look so solemn, little girl? Let us make this journey together. Give me your little hand; trust me; I will be good to you, and perhaps in the end, you will give me your shy little smile.

Actually, you will have not one but two lives: *before and after immigration.*

CHAPTER 2

War

Riva Gankin (née Zunz)

My mom always told me she knew I would be lucky. Even the odds of me being born at all were very slim. A horrible war devastated my parents' country. Millions of people were killed; entire families were destroyed. My parents lived in the Byelorussian city of Gomel at that time. The Nazis took Gomel six weeks after the beginning of the war. They captured the larger Minsk, where I was born many years later, almost immediately. Most people didn't have time to escape from there. Hundreds of thousands of Jews were murdered in the ghettos, most of them old people, women, and small children.

Before the war started, my parents managed to scrape some money together and bought a house, their first home.

Mom, Dad, and little Boris

Of course, it was small, almost tiny, but my mom painted both rooms white, and that immediately made them look clean and festive. She made curtains from her old skirt, light gray with tiny blue flowers, and my dad found them very pretty. They slept on the floor for a while, but they were young, so what did it matter?

They both worked and raised a child, my only brother. My dad went to college at night. I grew up hearing how he was always the best student, and how my brother was always the best, and how I would also get straight As one day. It was expected; nothing less would do.

Before the German invasion, people were told that the Soviet Red Army was strong, much stronger than Hitler's army. However, once the actual war started, the Germans kept getting closer and closer, and the bombings became worse every day. My dad had the option of staying with "his" factory which would exempt him from frontline service. The factory was working for the army from the beginning of the war, and they needed good people. However, he wanted to fight the Nazis.

Dad in military uniform

When I look at his pictures in uniform, they are touching and heartbreaking. They are also almost funny because it is hard to imagine a less soldierly man. From these pictures, a skinny young man with round eyeglasses and a huge forehead gently smiles at me—a man with a kind, scholarly face. It is hard to imagine him with a gun. It is impossible to picture him shooting at other people. It is tragic to know that, at times, people like him have to shoot to defend their families, their homes, and their country.

But was he shooting at "people"? Were the dark figures in the sight of his gun even human to him? How could they seem human when they had killed almost all of his family, including small children and old folks? Many of his relatives, including one brother, were killed fighting. He mourned them, but at least he knew why they died. But how could he come to terms with the murders of his elderly aunts and uncles, his cute little nieces and nephews, his mother? They became ashes in concentration camps, lines on modest monuments in various ghettos, bitter memories in his heart, and gray hair on his head. He carried this weight all his life on his slightly stooped shoulders.

What happened to him just after he was drafted indeed proves that Dad was not a typical warrior. I heard this story many times, always from my mom, so I will let her narrate it to you.

Do you know what happened next? They assigned him to a ski brigade. They planned to drop them from the sky on parachutes right where the Germans were, and they would ski and kill the Nazis left and right in close combat. What skis, I am asking you? Your dad had no idea how to ski. I am not sure if he knew what the skis were for. He wouldn't kill a chicken for the life of him. Can you tell me what he would do in close combat? The Nazis would kill him within seconds, even if he had managed to open his parachute in the first place, which I strongly doubt, by the way. Don't make faces. I love your dad more than you do, but trust me on this one.

Do you want to hear what happened next? Okay, I'll tell you, but only if you drink a glass of warm milk and eat a piece of bread with butter. Yes, the whole piece, and yes, with butter! I save this butter; even your brother eats it once a week and he is a child too, barely sixteen. I never even try it, and this princess doesn't want to eat it. No butter, no story! Don't keep food behind your cheek; you are not a camel. Chew, chew on it! Okay, you chew, and I talk, isn't it fair? Good girl.

So, where did I stop? Oh, yes, I was telling you how this great warrior was assigned to a ski brigade to jump from the sky onto the heads of Germans and save our motherland. Then a miracle happened. One big-shot general, a very decent man, came to check on his troops before sending them to die. He saw your dad, his nose and all, and he laughed. Why did he laugh? After you are done eating, I will show you the picture album. I know that you've seen it many times, but I want you to see Dad's picture wearing that military uniform again. Chew. Don't hold the bread behind your cheek. Okay, good girl, just chew and swallow. Don't forget to swallow!

So, this general looked at your dad, and he laughed and made some jokes about Dad's looks. He asked if your dad was going to kill Nazis with his nose instead of his bayonet. Your dad, of course, turned all red; you know how easily he blushes, like a sixteen-year-old girl. Yes, this was not a funny joke—even a four-year-old understands that—but one cannot talk back to a general, especially during the war. Your dad was ready to fall through the floor, but he couldn't do it, so he just stood there. Then the general spoke with him a little, asking about his family and his education. He asked if your dad could count. As you know, he is an accountant; of course he could count all right. Dad replied, and suddenly the general gave the order to transfer him to anti-tank artillery to do some calculations. Artillery was no resort either, but at least there were no skis and no parachutes. Can you imagine such incredible luck? Don't repeat my words to anyone, but I think this was the good old Jewish God intervening, even though I was taught not to believe in Him.

Mom was right—Dad could count. By the beginning of the war, he had already graduated from the Financial University in Moscow with honors, specializing in finance. He got a chance to survive, and, luckily, this chance worked.

CHAPTER 3

Evacuation

I remember by heart my mom's stories about their 1941 evacuation from Gomel.

> So, your dad was off to fight the Nazis, and we were put on a train and went far, far away, to Stalingrad on the Volga, where my brother Zalman was living. Stalingrad was so far to the east. Who could ever have guessed the Germans would be there soon? And you think it was a luxury train, wooden seats and all? No way. It was a freight train, and I felt so lucky to be on it, escaping the Nazis. People were storming the carriages, carrying their stuff with them, and I did too. I packed six suitcases—some linens, spoons, and the tablecloth. I also took all our clothes—your brother's and mine—not that we had too many. Fortunately, I also packed some family photos, and that is how they survived. How old was your brother? He was five, just a little older than you are now. He was such a good boy, and he ate very well, never keeping food behind his cheek. It's not that there was too much to eat anyway.

The train was going east. We were so lucky—the bombs didn't hit us. We saw other trains after they were bombed, and it was horrible. Also, Boris, your brother, was a healthy little boy; he didn't give me any trouble. Your favorite Auntie Pesya was on a different train with her little daughter, Anyechka, barely two, and the girl got scarlet fever and died. Such a tragedy! Look at me! Don't even think about crying. You didn't know her. Nothing for you to cry about. No, I am not crying; my eyes are itching, that's all. Milk? Okay, okay, later, but with bread.

First, we came to Stalingrad where your uncle worked as an engineer at a military plant. They were building tanks, and I remember him listening to the noise the tanks made and saying, "That's what we need; we need more of these." I thought I would stay there until the war was over. It was supposed to be our quick victory, wasn't it? Who would have thought they would make it to Volga?

Well, to make a long story short, I will just tell you that we almost missed the last boat from Stalingrad. It was a horrible journey, but finally, we arrived to a very distant place in the Ural Mountains.

When our train arrived in this city, Kurgan was its name, it was already cold there, and soon it was bitterly cold. The only good news was that my father, your grandfather Leib, and my sister Roza all reunited with us in Kurgan. Roza and I both worked at the same plant. It used to be a perfume factory before the war, but we quickly started making shells and landmines.

At work, they gave me a ration of bread and hot soup once a day, but I never ate this soup. I had a little thermos. I would keep this soup there and bring it home to your brother. Was he happy! He had his own ration of bread, but it was just a small piece. The child was growing, he needed something to eat, and he was always so hungry. I would bring him this soup and the part of bread I saved for him and my dad. Sometimes, especially on holidays, they would give us some porridge, and I would put it into the same thermos. We had to work long hours, but whenever I got home, I would always find little Boris waiting for me, and his food was still warm.

No, I could never leave work earlier: war, strict laws, and I could not be late even for one minute. Early in the morning, I would take your brother to day care. It was frequently raining and very muddy. Soon it was winter; often, the snow was too high, and he didn't have good boots. I had to carry him on my back for six blocks, and he was so heavy. Even now, I still don't understand why he was so heavy; he was only five, all skin and bones. Maybe it was because I was always hungry. I often thought I would collapse right there, and we would both freeze to death. Fortunately, it never happened.

Oh, and then one day there was a big snowstorm; the wind was so strong it nearly ripped my face. I tried to run, but I couldn't, and I was late for work. Do you know what they did with people who were late for work? Arrested them and sent them to labor camps, that's what! I was sure it was the end of me. However, I was so lucky. My boss at that time was a good woman. She died that same winter, may God rest her soul. She covered for me, saying that I went to the bank and was late for a good reason. What bank could

Roza Zunz

be open so early in the morning? It was such an obvious lie, but I was young, had a son, and my husband was at war, so everyone pretended to believe her. She saved not only me, but your brother too. Why did she save him too? If I were arrested, he would be sent to an orphanage and most likely die there from starvation.

I had always worked in accounting, but in the beginning of our Kurgan stay, I went to work at the assembly line. People who worked there were getting bigger rations of bread, which I could share with your brother and grandfather. Roza was an engineer, and thus received a bigger ration such as was allotted to the technical specialists. She also always shared it with us and sometimes even brought some sugar cubes for Boris. That boy loved sugar! And you, you never eat anything sweet. What a headache you are!

Somehow, we survived the whole winter. This first winter was the worst. Later, when the grass started growing, it became a little easier. I would go and pick stinging nettle leaves, dandelions—whatever I could find—boil them in water, and we had good soup, very healthy with lots of vitamins. Some days I was able to buy a potato to put into this soup, and it was so yummy. Oddly enough, dandelions don't taste that good now, when we have other food to eat. By the way, would you eat a small bowl of potato soup? It's very tasty, and I have some sour cream for you. Of course no, always no! You are spoiled. You don't appreciate all this luxury. Okay, in half an hour, but with bread.

Do you want to know what saved us later, in the fall? At work, they gave each of us a small patch of land outside of town and a sack of seed potatoes. The land was virgin, very tough, but we got a spade, and Roza and I planted these *potatoes. Of course, we didn't plant whole potatoes; it would be such a waste. I would peel the skin, together with a piece of potato, where the sprout was. I cooked what was left of the potatoes; it was such a feast. Then, in the fall, we got seven full sacks of it. Can you imagine such riches? We dug it out and brought the sacks home. I couldn't lift the whole sack; after all, I am 4'9" when I stand on tiptoes, and I was so skinny you could see right through me. I would fill maybe a third of it, and carry it on my back, just as I carried your brother. We had to hurry because the frost could come at any moment, and it would kill the crop. However, we were so lucky. We got it all to the cellar, and it sustained us until next spring. Of course, we had to be careful and make it last. We also had to save some to plant next fall. Nevertheless, we survived.*

When I was old enough to understand, Mom would hint to me that she could have had an easier life. She was young and pretty, and a married executive showed a lot of interest in her. With their husbands at war, some women were looking for somebody to support them, to provide security, or just to fill the need for romance and companionship in their lives. However, for her, it was always my dad, and only my dad.

She told me many times that, besides these potatoes, there was something else that kept her going. My dad's letters were her lifeline, her salvation in the darkest moments of hunger and despair. He wrote to her whenever he could. His letters were affectionate and warm. He also missed them, his wife and his son. Every evening, Mom read his new letters to little Boris, and he remembered them all his life.

Then, in 1942, when Dad was in Stalingrad, she did not get any letters from him for six weeks. Six long weeks—and she

Dad in 1944

got nothing, not a word. She read old letters to her son. It was easy to trick a five-year-old, but she was worried sick about her husband. She cried herself to sleep every night. So many women around her received death notifications (*pohoronka* in Russian), the most feared word during the war. Mom did all she could. She remembered some prayers her father taught her when she was a child. She prayed for him all the time, for him to survive the war. Even if he is maimed, just bring him back home to me, dear God, please bring him home. During these most difficult months, prayers helped her keep the hopes up. They taught her in Soviet school not to pray, but there are no atheists in foxholes. Her prayers worked. She found out that Dad's army had been surrounded in Stalingrad all this time. He wrote to her every day, but couldn't post his letters. She eventually got all of them in one day, and that day was probably one of the happiest of her life.

Whenever she got a letter from Dad, she was always in seventh heaven. Then she would look at the envelope and see that he posted it a month ago. So many bad things could have happened to him during this month. Throughout these long years, her joy was always intermixed with tears.

My dad told me later that one evening he was in his dugout writing a letter, and all of a sudden, it was as if some invisible hand made him bend. That very second, a shell fragment went right through where his head was a moment ago. During these almost four years, he participated in the Battle of Stalingrad and in the Battles of Kursk and Bucharest, all of them the bloodiest clashes of World War II. In 1944, he got a bad shell shock, then pneumonia on top of it, and had to spend six months in a hospital in Hungary. Mom's desperate prayers worked. Dad came back with all his limbs, almost the same as when he left, except his head was now full of gray hair. By the end of the war, he was thirty-two.

She told me many times that, besides these potatoes, there was *something else that kept her going.*

CHAPTER 4

My Dad's Family

Dad was not a very talkative man. He was an introvert, a trait I certainly inherited from him. And yet, many men much more outspoken than my dad were reluctant to talk about the war. For most of them, reliving their horrible experiences was painful even many years later. Some of them, though, had to endure another pain, probably an even greater one. It was the pain of losing their loved ones—not to disease, not to hunger, not to an accident but to the evil determination of individuals who called themselves human, even superhuman, beings. Dad only spoke to me about it once. I also know bits and pieces of his family tragedy from my mom, from other relatives, from the testimonies in Yad Vashem, as well as from a few of my dad's friends from the same town.

My dad was born in Shchedrin, a small town or shtetl in the Gomel province, not far from the city of Zhlobin in Belarus. I wish I knew more about his side of the family and very much regret that, when I was younger, I didn't know how to ask questions. Unfortunately, now there is no one left to ask.

My great-grandfather, Avrom-Ber, was a rabbi in Zhlobin. I have a family tree drawn by my uncle Evgeny Gankin. In this drawing,

Rabbi Avrom-Ber is the trunk of a big tree. Despite all the Nazis in the world, this tree is still growing.

I know very little about my paternal grandfather. Afroim-Mordukh Gankin was trained to be a rabbi, but became a shochet (ritual slaughterer), since the rabbi's position in the shtetl was already occupied by his older brother. He died in 1936 and did not live to see his wife, several children, and grandchildren perish in the Holocaust. His photos, if they even existed, did not survive the war either.

His oldest son and my dad's oldest brother Lev was a teacher and then, I believe, a school principal in Borisov, northeast of Minsk. He was killed by the Nazis, together with his wife Sonya and their two young children (my cousins) whose names I never knew. There are no photos, only the certificate from Yad Vashem.

David, Manya, and Aron Gankin (1932)

Dad's second brother, David Gankin, was an engineer. He was evacuated with his family, but one of his children got sick and they got off the train in the city of Vyazma to seek medical care for him. Vyazma was unexpectedly taken by German paratroopers, and David, his wife Beila, and their two small children were all killed in the ghetto. By that time, he was thirty-two.

Abram Gankin

Abram Gankin, the youngest of all brothers, was born in 1918 and was an engineer. He lived in the city of Gorky (Nizhny Novgorod) in Russia. He fought in the war and was listed as missing in action.

The beautiful young woman in this picture is my aunt Basya. She died during the war of mycotoxicosis after eating bread made from poisonous grain.

Margolis, Basya, Aron, and Evgeny Gankin

Two other sisters, Minya and Manya (Mihlya), survived the war. I knew both of them. They were both very kind, though both had difficult lives. Aunt Manya survived not just the war, but also two personal tragedies. Her older son was killed in the Soviet Army in the fifties, and her husband died the same year in a traffic accident. Her younger son (one of my favorite cousins), Misha Vayner, lives in Israel, as do my other cousins both on my mom's and on my dad's sides.

Minya and Manya (Mihlya) Gankin

CHAPTER 5

My Grandmother Margolis

Margolis Gankin (circa 1930)

This is a picture of my grandmother Margolis Gankin (née Pinsky). When the war started, she lived in Shchedrin alone. All eight of her children had left the place for bigger cities and greater opportunities. When the Germans approached, she did not want to leave her house and run. She was almost sixty—an old woman in her own eyes. Whatever she had there—her house, chickens, not much else—was precious to her. Besides, German soldiers had stayed in her house during World War I. Those Germans were civil, gave chocolate to the kids, and she, like many others around, dismissed the rumors of recent German atrocities as Bolshevik propaganda. She decided to stay, and so did many other people. Their able-bodied men who could be seen as a problem for the occupation were all in the Red Army fighting Nazis anyway. They were sure that no one would touch old folks, women, or small children. They expected hunger, difficult times. Who could have predicted what really happened?

When I was still a toddler, a young man came to visit my dad. This man was probably no more than fourteen in 1942. He was one of the very few, possibly the only one, from the Shchedrin ghetto who survived. I believe on the day of the final massacre he escaped and was very lucky to have been accepted by the partisans. In November of 1942, Moscow sent a radiogram to commanders of partisan formations, forbidding the admission of surviving Jews into their units. This order led to the death of thousands of Jews who miraculously escaped from the ghettos and were ready to fight. By that time, specifically Jewish partisan groups were forming in Belarus's forests, and this young man may have joined one of them.

The Nazis started with those whom they deemed unable to work. First, they rounded up old people and small children, took them to the synagogue, poured gasoline at the corners, and set the building on fire. The synagogue was in a small wooden house. It went up in flames very quickly.

The final liquidation of the Shchedrin ghetto happened on March 8, 1942. The Nazis came. They rounded up all the remaining Jews, took them to the Jewish cemetery, and killed them. My father told me that he lost forty of his close relatives— his aunts, uncles, cousins, and their small children—on that day, not counting the more distant family members. Altogether, more than two thousand Jews were murdered on a single day. The Shchedrin ghetto, which had functioned for eight months, ceased to exist.

Margolis Gankin (artist: Evgeny Gankin)

I was born several years after the Second World War. My parents named me after my grandmother Margolis. They often told me that I have her shy smile, and when I am sad or scared, I cover my mouth exactly the way she did. I am very sorry I never met her. I always felt that not knowing both my grandmothers has robbed me of something very important. I probably missed the unconditional love only a grandmother can give. I inherited nothing from her, except a gesture and a smile. I never even visited the village where the Nazis murdered her.

Then why do I think so often about her, why do I look every day at her portrait? In this portrait, drawn by her son Evgeny Gankin, she is engulfed in flames, covering her mouth with that very familiar gesture. Am I more aware of being Jewish because of her horrible fate? Did it make me more attuned to the dangers of anti-Semitism, of any hate? I do not know, but in my genes, in my genetic memory, there is definitely a horror of her death. With my parents and my brother gone, I am now the witness to her memory, and when I am gone, my children and grandchildren will carry this weight.

I remember very well how my dad and his landsmen were collecting money for the monument to the victims of Shchedrin ghetto. It was a simple black monument which was finished in 1963, and the inscription on it honored the murdered Jews of Shchedrin in two languages: Russian and Yiddish. I also remember that one woman, who unfortunately was also Jewish and whose relatives were in the same mass grave, wrote a complaint either to the Communist Party authorities or to the KGB, denouncing the actions of the Shchedrin survivors as Jewish nationalism. The Yiddish inscription disappeared, as did any explicit mention of the victims as Jews. Instead, it honored the "peaceful inhabitants" who were killed in Shchedrin.

Today this monument has an inscription in three languages: Russian, Yiddish, and English.

I would rather not write these last paragraphs, but I am afraid I should. The survivor of the Shchedrin massacre also told my parents what I call the story of the Shabbos goy. This story is hard to comprehend and even harder to put into writing. A Shabbos goy is a gentile who goes from one Jewish home to another on Shabbat, doing things a religious Jew cannot do on this holy day of rest. Such a person knows everyone in the shtetl, and usually his or her relationship with Jewish neighbors is good or even friendly.

When the Nazis, at gunpoint, were taking Jews to the cemetery for what was to be their final walk, final breath of fresh air, and final prayer, desperate mothers were trying to hide their kids, at least the little ones, the favorite ones, the babies. This Shabbos goy entered the houses along with the soldiers and collaborationist policemen, counted the children, and would often say, "Moishele is not here. Yankele is missing." She helped the murderers find the hidden children and bring them to their deaths.

After the war, the house of this woman was full of meager Jewish possessions. My father saw his family's Shabbat candlesticks on her windowsill. The survivors talked to the Soviet police, but no one was interested in bringing her to justice. One can only hope that she got justice in another world.

CHAPTER 6

My Grandfather Leib Zunz

Sitting: Leib, Hanna; Standing: Zalman, and Isaac Zuntz (circa 1920)

I hope that one day my grandkids will read this book. I certainly wish that their most pressing issue would not be how to remain human in a world ruled by inhumanity. They were lucky enough to be born to good parents in a good country. Still, times and circumstances change. It is easier to survive knowing that you are not alone, that behind you there is a long line of decent and brave people.

I do not remember seeing my grandfather for the first time, but my mom never let me forget that I threw a tantrum and screamed, "Go away, old man with a beard!" In my own defense, I have to say that I was not yet two at the time, and that he certainly looked very different from all the other men I usually saw. In the fifties, all Soviet men were dressed the same way. They usually wore almost identical dark-colored suits, boring ties, and wide-brimmed hats. Their faces were clean-shaven, and they all sported identical haircuts.

My grandfather was an Orthodox Jew who looked and dressed in accordance with his beliefs and traditions. He had a long gray beard which he never cut. He always covered his head and wore a long dark coat with fringes showing underneath. As I grew up, I learned to appreciate his knowing look of a sage, his kind and wise twinkling eyes.

In tough times, when the government persecuted all religions, Leib Zunz held a daily minyan (prayer) in his home. I still recall the faces of the men who came to pray in the evening, all of them wearing hats and all of them with long beards. I remember a man my mom called Reb Girsh, a shochet, with a dignified face and nice, refined features. I remember simple faces, wise faces, more and less polished manners, clean clothes, shabby clothes. These men got together every night to pray, to fulfill their religious obligations. There were no young men there, only old people, the remnants of the not so distant past. To any observer, their faith would seem to be on the verge of dying. Yet, it survived the Soviet times too.

Though throughout his life he strictly observed Jewish law, Granddad understood that the Soviet regime made it extremely difficult to avoid work on Shabbat and to abide by the dietary laws. His last several years were spent in Minsk, in our one-bedroom apartment. By that time, my brother was married and living with his wife at her parents' place. My grandfather shared the bedroom with me. My parents, as usual, slept on a sofa in the living room.

Our household, though emphatically Jewish, was not kosher. Mom kept three separate sets of dishes for my grandfather: one for dairy food, one for meat, and one for Passover. He ate meat only on Jewish holidays, when it was possible to find a shochet at the farmers market. My mom kept his food on a separate shelf in the refrigerator.

My grandfather knew that the rest of the family ate whatever Mom was able to buy that day. When I grew up, I started appreciating his tolerance. He certainly was unhappy with our way of life, but he never showed it. He told me once that he was grateful to me for bringing friends home and not being ashamed of his strange looks. Later, I found out why he almost never went for a walk or ventured outside to sit in the small garden in the yard. When not protected by the walls of our apartment, he was always mocked by children and scorned by adults. I was twelve when he came to live with us, and I suspect that he also thought his appearances outside would make my life more difficult.

Wise and spiritual, my grandfather possessed a mysterious ability to foresee the future. My cousin from Leningrad drowned in Ukraine, far away from anyone he knew. His parents received the notification of his death simultaneously with the letter from my granddad, in which he consoled them for their tragic loss. The letter from Gomel, Belarus, was postmarked on the day the tragedy happened. There was never any explanation; he just knew.

The family lore is full of similar stories. He saved his oldest son during Stalin's purges by making him throw away his radio the day before the KGB, responding to an anonymous denunciation that he was listening to foreign radio stations, knocked on his door. All the children and grandchildren, most of them intellectuals and skeptics, nonetheless believed him to be their guardian and protector even after his death. Both my brother and I named our own kids after him.

These days, we all know things that give religion a bad name. Leib Zunz, of blessed memory, gave it a good name, and I am always grateful to him for this. I also believe that he has made me a little better and a little stronger.

There was never
any explanation;
he just knew.

CHAPTER 7

My Grandmother Hannah

My grandmother Hannah was a rabbi's daughter. Of course she was. Children of rabbis usually married children of other rabbis. I know exactly who my husband would be if I had been born eighty years earlier. As it is, my husband is the next best thing—he is a professor. This is a bit of a joke, but I would probably make a professor out of anyone who married me.

Hannah Zunz (née Komissarova)

I have a picture of Hannah's father, the only picture of all my great-grandparents. I know just one detail about him, but it is worth mentioning. When pogroms were ravaging

Boruch Komissarov (circa 1890)

Jewish shtetls, he went to speak with the local priest. This priest gave a touching sermon to his flock, and their shtetl stayed calm; there were no pogroms there.

I also heard the story about him approving of his grandkids having a good secular education. With his blessing, his grandchildren (my uncles) went to a good secondary school in Gomel. He said, "If not rabbis, let them become lawyers or doctors and give good money to charity [tzedakah]."

Sitting: Sarah Zunz, Pesya Zunz, Hannah Zunz; Standing: Hanaan Zunz, Grigory Berin, Riva Gankin, Aron Gankin, Roza Zunz, Zalman Zunz (circa 1935–1936)

My grandmother Hannah did not have an easy life. She married a Jewish scholar and provided for her family while he dedicated his life to studying the Torah and Talmud. Before the 1917 revolution, she owned a small leather goods store and worked in it. She also gave birth to six children and raised them all to adulthood. It was not trivial at that time—child and infant mortality in Russia at the beginning of the twentieth century was extremely high. Five of her children are in this picture: Hanaan (Honya), Zalman, Pesya, Roza, and my mom. The three kids in the picture are the children of Honya and Sarah: Aron, Nina, and Ilya. Pesya is holding her infant son, Joel, in her lap. My parents had recently married, and my brother Boris had not been born yet, but my mom is already pregnant with him.

Two of Hanna's children, Zalman and Roza, became engineers; three others, including my mom, were accountants. One of the sons, my uncle Isaac, is not in this family photo, and for a very good reason. At the time this picture was taken, he was far away, in a different country.

The handsome man in this picture was a rebel. He did not observe the religious rules of the house, and at eighteen, he became a Zionist. As Stalin grew more and more powerful, being a member of any party or movement except the Communist Party became a crime. Eventually, Isaac was arrested, tried, and sentenced to hard labor in Siberia. He would never have seen freedom again and most likely would have been killed during the purges of 1937, or later. Fortunately, Hannah Zunz, his mother, saved his life. I don't know

Isaac and Hannah Zunz (née Margalit)

how this very religious, provincial woman managed it, but she went to Moscow and got an audience with Mikhail Ivanovich Kalinin, who for many years was the nominal head of state of the Russian Soviet Federative Socialist Republic and later of the Soviet Union. She persuaded Kalinin to modify Isaac's sentence. Instead of going to Siberia, Isaac was exiled from the country.

Uncle Isaac went to what was then called Palestine. He married the beautiful woman in the photo, Hannah Margalit, who in marriage became an exact namesake of his mother and raised four children with her. He also helped build his country, Israel.

I remember very well the picture of two handsome young men, one of them in a military uniform. They were my first cousins and the sons of Isaac Zunz, but they looked very different. They were free men, and somehow it was obvious, even to the young me— the girl who did not see too many free people.

I finally met my cousins in 1996, when I visited Israel for the first time. I liked them a lot, and I am sorry that I never got to meet my uncle Isaac.

Grandmother Hannah would eventually have thirteen grandchildren, but she did not live to see all of them. She died suddenly of a heart attack at the age of fifty-eight in 1940.

Boris and me with the Zunzes; Seated next to us: Jonathan, Ora, and Ofra; Standing: Roza (wife of Jonathan), Dov (2017)

CHAPTER 8

More About My Parents

My mom had a very strong personality. If, as in the famous joke, the main difference between a terrorist and a Jewish mother is that you can negotiate with the terrorist, then my mom was the ultimate Jewish mother. Before I got married, almost nothing was open to discussion, not food, nor clothing, nor my

My parents (circa 1965)

curfew. Every attempt to disagree she met with "Of course, if I say it's black, you say it's white," and that was the end of the conversation.

At home, Mom was most certainly the boss. She handled all practical matters. She had good hands and knew not only how to cook and sew, but also how to repair a broken electric iron and a leaking faucet, how to build furniture, and how to wallpaper and paint. In everyday life, she treated Dad like a small child. She often said that if Dad needed to hammer a nail into the wall, he would drive it headfirst. She handled money, made vacation plans, purchased what was necessary, and took care of the sick. She had enough energy to heat a small town.

Dad was very gentle and very impractical. He seldom argued with her or with anyone else. At the same time, their relationship was not one of a shrewish wife and a henpecked husband. Looking back, I realize that she loved and respected him too much to bully him. My 5'5" tall, narrow-boned, skinny dad seemed tall and broad-shouldered to Mom. She respected his judgments, his religious beliefs, his spirituality, his tenderness.

Mom was a drama queen. She never suffered in silence, always exaggerated her woes, and the world was mostly black-and-white to her. She was a strong-willed woman, sometimes judgmental, with a great sense of humor. Dad always downplayed things, always found excuses for everyone and explanations for everything. For better or worse, I inherited my dad's personality. Because of him, or possibly because of my mom, I became a self-proclaimed member of what I call the Men's Defense League, which was a stroke of luck for my husband and probably not that good for me.

Despite his gentle personality, when things were important to my dad, to his conscience, he stuck to his guns, and no one, not even Mom, could do anything about it. It was very unusual for an officer of the Red Army during the war not to become a member of the Communist Party. He somehow managed it. His career seriously suffered from the lack of party membership. That did not matter to him. I cannot imagine him doing something he considered morally wrong. I also never saw my bossy mom harass him about the things he considered important.

Dad was not involved in any anti-Soviet activity, but he really disliked the Communist Party and the Soviet government. When he saw the especially nasty members of the politburo or various general secretaries of the Communist Party on TV, he would always say, *"Yimakh shemo ve zikhro* (וְזִכְרוֹ יִמַּח שְׁמוֹ)," which translates as "May his name and his memory be erased." Dad hardly ever cursed, but Wikipedia states that Yimakh shemo is one of the strongest curses in the Hebrew language.

Dad never taught me any Hebrew. It was dangerous to teach Hebrew; people were arrested and sent to labor camps for this, even in my time. Recently, I learned from my sister that he, nevertheless, did teach one young man the language of the Torah (for free, of course). For conspiracy's sake, my parents called this man "a nephew" on the phone.

Dad taught me to read Yiddish, though, and I read the wonderful bittersweet stories of Sholem Aleichem in the original language.

Both my parents believed in charity, in tzedakah, and in their poorest times, they always found people who were worse off than they were. They found them, and they helped them. They were both very pro-Jewish and pro-Israel. At home, Dad was always listening to foreign radio stations, including the Voice of America and Kol Israel. He often took his radio set with him to bed, and Mom nicknamed it "his second wife." That second wife was even noisier than the first one, since broadcasts coming from capitalist countries were very frequently jammed, replacing the voice of the announcer with an ear-piercing sound. Mom did not like the competition but tolerated it.

Mom often said that she would like to die before Dad, that she did not want to live without him. It sounded a bit melodramatic, very consistent with her usual drama queen behavior. Later events proved that she really meant it.

Dad died unexpectedly. My birthday in 1985 happened right after Yom Kippur, the Day of Atonement. Dad was very happy that evening. He spent the whole of Yom Kippur in his synagogue, fasting, leading the services, and praying. At his funeral, the family found out that after the death of the rabbi, Dad was the only one left who remembered how to lead the services. Dad was very modest, and never mentioned this to any of us.

On my birthday, Dad looked unusually happy. He said that he was sure all those whom he loved would have a great year. I was eight months pregnant, and uncharacteristically, my very reserved dad suddenly told me that, much as they loved me, they loved my daughter Lena even more and would be so happy to welcome another baby into the family soon.

The next day, Dad left their apartment to visit us. His heart suddenly stopped. The neighborhood children found him, but when the ambulance arrived, he was already dead. In death, my long-nosed, very Jewish-looking dad was beautiful, just as Mom always saw him. Mom outlived him by ten years, but in reality, she died with him. Since the day Dad passed away, she was never the same. She wandered empty-eyed from room to room, talking only about him and blaming everyone for his death.

Children usually don't see romance in their parents' lives. Only many years later I realized that theirs was a real love story.

CHAPTER 9

Baking Matzah

When I was little, we had a neighbor who spent all her days making the rounds, starting with the first apartment and finishing her day by visiting the last one. Her favorite topics were the numerous virtues of her only son and the even more numerous horrible shortcomings of her daughter-in-law. I do not know if the Guinness World Records considers incessant chatting as a record-setting achievement, but this woman would be a serious contender for a talking championship.

Usually, when a man leaves his wife after twenty-five years of marriage, it creates an uproar among neighbors. In the case of her husband, everyone bought into his argument that even murderers were often paroled after twenty-five years. Mom was sure that his next wife would be a mute.

One day I remember so well started with the warning that if this neighbor or anyone else came to visit, we could not open the door. We had to pretend that no one was home. Mom told me that we would be doing something unusual, something very special. We would be baking special bread called matzah. Mom told me to memorize the recipe just in case. "You just have to take the flour and add water until you have a soft dough. Like this, see? Knead it for about five minutes. God willing, when you grow up, you won't need to bake it yourself; it will be sold everywhere, though it doesn't look very likely now."

She explained that we should do it very fast to prevent the dough from rising, because our forefathers did it this way. I liked the word *forefathers*, but what really fascinated me was the small wheel with very sharp teeth. Mom let me make holes in the matzah with it.

When I grew up, I never had to bake matzah. By the time I got married and had my own family, it became possible to buy it at the synagogue, a small wooden house attended by a handful of old men. At that time, the Soviet government still did not approve of buying and selling matzah, but did not arrest people for doing so either. These days, I just go to the nearest supermarket and select the flavor and the manufacturer I like.

Although I never had to bake matzah myself, whenever I see it, I recall that small wheel which fascinated me when I was four. I can still feel it in my hands, remember the mix of excitement and fear I felt that day. I still look up to this tiny woman, who was terrified of mice and thunderstorms but somehow found the courage to bake matzah in 1953 and to trust her four-year-old daughter with this perilous secret.

We had to pretend that *no one was home.*

CHAPTER 10

The Apartment

The apartment chronicle is my mom's story. Let us listen to her.

You want to know why else I think you are lucky. Sure, I will tell you. When we came to Minsk after the war, the whole city was in ruins. Your dad had found a good job at the Ministry of Forestry and Wood Industry, and he got a room in the same apartment building where we are now. The room was tiny. I have never been to prison, thank God, but that's how I imagine a prison cell. Three steps in each direction, more or less. Still, we were happy. After all these years of war, we were alive, and we were together. Of course, we had to use the outhouse even during the winter, and the stove didn't heat even our tiny room all that well. To use a woodburning stove, you need to have enough wood, don't you?

Nevertheless, we were so much more comfortable than during the war, and your dad was with us. By 1947, all ration cards were abolished. No one likes standing in lines for hours to buy food, but if you can buy bread, potatoes, and sometimes milk and butter, you really should not complain.

Then my sister Pesya moved to Minsk. She was divorced. Her daughter had died. All she had was her son and us. Of course, later on, Dad helped her get a job and a room to live in, but at that time, the two of them moved in with us. Where were we sleeping? Dad and I slept on our narrow bed, two boys under the bed, Pesya on the floor—the more, the merrier. Many people told us we were crazy. We could barely move in our room even without two more people. This is all true, but to stay human, we have to help each other. See, you are nodding. This is obvious even to a four-year-old. Besides, it was only for six months or so.

I always thought that one kid was not enough. I wanted a girl with curly hair and a big bow on top, just like you. When good God granted me my wish and I knew we would have a baby, I was the happiest woman in the universe. I was not exactly a spring chicken by then, at thirty-six years old, and I didn't spend most of these years at a resort either. How long could we have waited to have a baby—until I was eighty? Anyway, I was so happy, and Dad was happy too. I spent nights sewing you cloth diapers, and cute tiny hats, everything I could think of. I was smiling all the time. We survived the war, and we were going to have a baby! Life was perfect.

I had it all figured out—you were going to sleep on the bed during the day and on the table at night. Again, people called us crazy, but you have to live your own life. If you know you are doing the right thing, you don't have to listen to other people. Naturally, all moms are different. You always have to listen to your mom, always, because she wishes you well, and she knows better. Even when you are my age, you'll have to listen to me. Agreed? Good girl! Of course, asking you to eat something now would be pushing my luck too far, wouldn't it? I knew it.

When you were about to be born, Dad walked me to the hospital. I stayed there, and Dad went to work. Then, unbelievably, a miracle happened. The head of the ministry (for brevity's sake, I will call him the Minister) called Dad into his office and told him that they had decided to give him a bigger room, almost three times as big as ours. Dad was in seventh heaven, of course, but before he became too happy, the Minister told him that he, I mean the Minister, had a big heart, didn't know how to say "no," and that's why he couldn't refuse when another man, a certain Maxim Isaakovich—who was occupying a different room of the same communal apartment with his daughter—also asked him about moving into "our" room. As a result, two families technically had the right to live in this room, except our competitors already had a big enough room and just two people living there, Uncle Maxim and his meshuggener (crazy) daughter Sonya, while we were four people jammed into a tiny roomlet. The Minister wished Dad good luck. What could your dad do? He thanked the Minister and left, wondering how in the world he was going to get into this bigger room before the people already living in the same apartment.

Now, if you eat a piece of bread with butter, I will tell you the rest of the story. Yes, with butter. Don't argue with me. Of course, you are hungry, and of course, I know better whether you are hungry or not. No butter, no story! You see, you can be good when you want to be! Open your mouth and don't forget to chew.

Then, when your dad came home, a second miracle happened. The woman who was vacating the room of our dreams approached him. She told him that she knew about our horrible living conditions. She felt very sorry for us, especially with the new baby about to be born. She told your dad that she would open the apartment door for him at two in the morning. The neighbors would be fast asleep, and Dad and your brother could move in. Can you imagine? At 2:00 a.m., like thieves, under the cover of darkness, and your dad is always so proper. Honestly, I have no idea how he survived all this.

Anyway, they moved in. In the morning, when Sonya saw Boris in the communal kitchen, she called him all kinds of names. Which names? No, I am not going to repeat them in front of you; believe me, none of them were good. She didn't say, "Dear Boris, I am so glad you have occupied the room which we thought would be ours." She didn't even say, "I am sorry you did it, but I understand why. Let's be good neighbors." She was a spoiled brat four years ago, and she still is. Her dad, Uncle Maxim Isaakovich, was more courteous. What do you expect from a man who graduated from the Sorbonne? He is a very smart man, and his life was not a picnic either.

It may seem hard to believe, but my parents and Maxim Isaakovich became good friends, and I think he was one of the most amazing people I met in my early childhood.

This new room changed many things for my parents. When they brought me home, they had a space for a small crib. Boris didn't sleep on the floor anymore. Eighteen square meters (194 square feet) at that time was a luxury. I do remember this room, and I remember that there were always people staying in it with us. Close and distant relatives, relatives of friends, and friends of relatives—all of them could find a soft place on the floor or a cot in times when hotels were available only to a selected few. There was also a meager dinner to share with us. Some of these people remained friends with our family forever.

My adult life started in a different era. When I got married, my husband, Boris, and I had a room in my parents' two-bedroom apartment. My little sister occupied the smaller of the two bedrooms. We had the bigger one, also eighteen square meters. We didn't have to rent a tiny room from a drunk who needed extra money, as some of our friends did. We got the bigger bedroom. My parents, as always, slept on a sofa in the living room.

With tiny Lena

Three years later, when our older daughter Lena was born, there was a place for her crib in our room. Lena did not sleep well, and I spent nights standing near her bed trying to soothe her, or holding her

Little Lena

in my arms. Once, completely exhausted, I decided to let her cry. Five minutes later, the door to our bedroom opened and in marched my mom in her nightgown. "You are not a mother; you are a wicked stepmother," declared my mom, obviously disgusted with me. This was the end of my feeble attempt to sleep-train Lena.

I married when I was twenty, and we finally got our own apartment when I was twenty-eight. Lena was five by then. I was working, and during the day, Mom was in charge of her meals. Of course, Lena was a chubby kid. I never made our kids eat more than they wanted, so after we moved away, she quickly shed the extra pounds. Mom, of course, was very, very unhappy with me.

For eight years, whenever our friends came to visit, we would all eat and drink tea in my parents' small kitchen. Many people just showed up unannounced, but there was always dinner in my mom's fridge for a guest, even if sometimes it was just some herring with boiled potatoes.

Today, in our big house with its formal dining room, we still often entertain close friends in the kitchen. In my mind, it is the warmest and coziest place of all. Our American friends started calling their kitchen the "Russian room" because we always tend to congregate there. These days, no one is asleep in the living room behind a thin wall, but I still automatically shush my husband when he is too loud.

I wanted a girl with curly hair and a big bow on top,
just like you.

CHAPTER 11

Book Burning

In 1949, Stalin started a campaign against "rootless cosmopolitans." In reality, this term was just a euphemism for Jews, which implied that Jews did not love their country and did not have any loyalty to it. For people like my dad, who had just come back from the war, who risked their lives every day to defend their country, it was a rude awakening. For many other Jews, who believed in the "brotherhood of nations" in the Soviet Union, it was even worse. Once again, the authorities reminded Jewish people that they were different from everyone else. Many Jews were accused of being traitors and spies and were arrested, tortured, and often killed.

Yiddish was the first language of my mom and dad, the language spoken by their parents and their parents' parents. Mom and Dad learned to speak Russian from their neighbors, friends, and at school. They were really bilingual and spoke Russian very well, without any "Jewish" accent. When I was a child, they always spoke Russian at home and used Yiddish to hide things from me. This, of course, didn't work very well. I learned to understand it perfectly and to appreciate its colorfulness and bittersweet humor.

Both of my parents spoke very rich, idiomatic Yiddish and could read and write in it too. Dad also knew biblical Hebrew, since in his childhood he studied in a yeshiva and trained to become a rabbi, but Hebrew books were very hard to come by. He knew Yiddish literature well and really enjoyed it. The names of Sholem Aleichem and Mendele Mocher-Sforim were often mentioned in our home.

Our small apartment was always full of books, mostly in Russian, but Yiddish books were also well-represented on our bookshelves. There was a huge respect for the written word, so burning books was an unimaginably heartbreaking task. Unfortunately, there was a good reason to do it. One of our neighbors, motivated either by her anti-Semitism or by a simple desire to improve her living conditions, wrote a letter to the KGB in 1952, denouncing my father as a Jewish nationalist and a British spy. My parents knew her name (I still remember it) and had to live on the same floor with her for three more years.

The KGB people called Dad's boss to their office and told him that he had to sign a similar letter. This man showed unbelievable courage and refused to do it.

My dad was not a big fish, so his boss was not tortured. Still, the KGB image was so horrible that not many people would have had the guts to do what this man did. More than that, he warned my dad about the danger. Since both of them knew that even walls at that time had ears, he met Dad in the hallway at work and told him in Hebrew, "Watch out. Be a father to your children."

Both Mom and Dad were frantic, but Mom was a woman of action. She would do whatever it took to save her husband. Without telling my dad, she burned all his Yiddish books. I don't know if the following monologue is real or it just seems to me that I remember it word for word, but I'll let my mom tell you about that day.

> I thought you were asleep. I tucked you in long ago. I don't know what to do with this girl. You ask her to eat—she stores food behind her cheek, saves it for hungry times, I guess. You ask her to drink milk—expect a fountain. You ask her to sleep tight because you need some privacy, and here she is, her eyes round and long ears pricked up.
>
> Well, there is something urgent I have to do. It cannot wait. I wish we had at least a warm toilet where one could lock a nosy child. Stop wailing; no one is locking you anywhere.
>
> Do you see these books? Do you see the letters? They don't look like Russian letters, do they? That's because they are not Russian. These books are in Yiddish. Yiddish is a language, like Russian. My family spoke it at home, and your dad's family too. Of course, I can read it; it was the first language I learned. These are good books too— Sholem Aleichem, Mendele Mocher-Sforim. I am about to do something I never thought I would have to do. This is about saving your dad. Oy s'iz shver tsu zayn a Yid (It's hard to be a Jew). How can one explain to an innocent child that people can be arrested and shot just for reading books in their native language in their own homes?
>
> Listen, I want you to forget what I am about to do. You know that I love books. We always buy books, even when we cannot afford it. It breaks my heart, but I am going to burn them right now in front of my child. I love books, but I love my husband more. When they come to check, we'll have only Russian books. We will have Tolstoy, Chekhov, and selected works of Marx and Lenin which they made your dad buy.

You know what? Don't listen to me. Remember it! Always
remember what they made me do! Tell your children about
it! Tell your children and grandchildren but not a word to the
neighbors, or your friends. Not a word to a living soul. Do you
hear me? The only people you can tell about it are your kids.
With a life like this, I'll most likely be dead by then anyway.

Mom, that's what I am doing now. I am telling your grandchildren and great-grandchildren about this.

Later, I learned that Mom also ripped the wires off our ancient radio set, which my dad and brother had recently brought home from a flea market.

Several days later, someone knocked on our door. My brother remembered two identically dressed men, wearing felt hats and dark gray overcoats. They entered our room without as much as saying hello to Mom. Mom was a genius—they started with the bookshelf. The works of the founders of Marxism-Leninism now took the most prominent place on it. Russian classics meekly flanked them.

Not finding anything criminal on the bookshelf, they decided to dig deeper. "Does your husband often listen to foreign radio stations?" they asked my terrified mom.

"This junk doesn't work," Mom replied casually. "We were planning to repair it, but still don't have the money to pay for it."

The men peeked inside the radio and took notice of our rough furniture, which was mostly made by my mom. They certainly noticed my brother's shaking lips and the milk-white face and the burning eyes of my mom, who was holding me in her arms the whole time. They left. This story has no continuation.

Actually, the previous paragraph is a lie. I realize that in it I am subconsciously making a feeble attempt to humanize them. I don't think that—in their line of work—these creeps ever felt sorry for anyone. They arrested people, old and young—people with children and childless people, sick people, dying people. They tortured them when so ordered. They killed them with the stroke of their pen, with their verdicts, with their bullets. Millions perished in the Gulag, and millions more were exiled to remote areas of the USSR. I don't know why my family was spared. My mom liked to think that it was her quick wit. My grandfather was sure that his prayers saved us. My dad credited his boss for this wonder. Anyway, a miracle happened and Dad was never arrested.

There was a huge respect for the written word, so burning books was an *unimaginably heartbreaking task.*

CHAPTER 12

My Brother

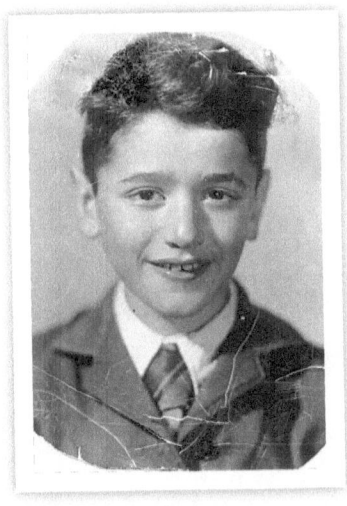

Boris

In 2008, I lost my only brother Boris to cancer. This little boy, who survived the war, whom my mom carried on her back during the bitterly cold Ural winters, grew up to become a very multifaceted man, a real polymath. He was an accomplished engineer and a talented inventor, with many patents to his name. He loved mountains and, as a group leader, took many people on hiking trips with him. He had an amazing talent for seeing beauty in every aspect of life, from the beauty of nature to the beauty of human love. This talent made him a poet.

He published many books of verse, and his poetic voice only became stronger with age. *He never lost his almost* childlike delight in the droplets of water on a leaf, in trees covered in snow, in an autumn forest, in life. He was an optimist and always saw the best in others.

Being a poet made him emotional and vulnerable, and he could easily exaggerate a slight discomfort or a minor illness. When a horrible disease struck, he amazed all of us with his courage, with his quiet acceptance of fate, with his patience, with final acts of selflessness. For a long time, I visited him almost every day in the hospital. I knew him well, and yet, I did not know him at all. The man I saw was a much bigger man than I could ever have guessed.

Family

In these last months, there were moments of heartbreaking beauty, when his love for his wife and sons was so obvious and so perfect. There was time to say goodbye, and I will be forever grateful for this. This chapter is but one more attempt on my part, probably very inadequately, to say that I loved him—my short tribute to his memory.

Returning to my childhood, I remember a young and handsome Boris who was very charismatic and very interested in girls. He wrote romantic poems, usually dedicated to his latest love interest. Unlike me, he was athletic and loved volleyball and basketball. Like me, he was an avid reader.

During his school years, boys and girls studied in separate schools. Coeducation was restored only in 1954. Our small apartment was always full of skinny, noisy boys—his classmates. I remember my mom slicing bread and sprinkling it with sugar. The ever-hungry teenagers greeted these "luxurious" sandwiches with wild enthusiasm. They all treated me like their own little sister. When I was sixteen, they would make me blush by telling me stories about babysitting and potty training me.

Boris wanted to be a physicist, but for a Jew to be admitted to the best university in 1954 was still impossible. He enrolled in the Belarusian Technological University (Technological Institute, in his time) and unexpectedly acquired a profession he actually liked.

My brother and his friends belonged to a very tough generation. As kids, they survived the war. Many of them lost their parents either in the war or during Stalin's purges.

His wartime childhood influenced his poetry and his personality. The memories of cold, of hunger, of Mom's tears were always with him. When he was dying, our daughter Lena came to say goodbye to him. He spent a day talking to her about his life. On that day, he remembered an episode when, while in the Urals, they got a letter from our dad, in which he mentioned that on a certain day his military train would be passing through Kurgan. Mom could take only one day off work a month, and on this day, they went to the railway station and waited. The trains with soldiers were going east. It was very cold, it was getting dark, and they could not even distinguish faces anymore. They were very tired and very miserable, when all of a sudden they heard someone screaming "Rivka!" and saw our dad on a quickly passing carriage's step, hanging on to the handrails. The dying seventy-one-year-old Boris called this one of the happiest moments of his life.

When Boris and his friends entered adulthood, Jews were widely discriminated against. Many people of his generation became the so-called *shestidesiatniki*, the sixties' generation, a subset of Soviet intelligentsia which participated in the liberal movement during the political *thaw* in the early 1960s. Disillusioned, some of them later left the country and the culture they loved so much. Such was the fate of my brother.

He and his wife Rita came to the United States in 1996, following their sons Michael and Leo. At that time, he was sixty. It was not simple to leave an old life behind, especially when that life was so rich and fulfilling. We worried about him, but he managed to start a new life, also meaningful and rewarding. He wrote and published poetry, and earned multiple awards.

Boris Gankin, 2007

Many years ago, he introduced me and many other people to the mountains. Now, in this new life, he took people to museums and nature, introducing them to the culture of his new land. He enriched the lives of many Russian immigrants, especially older people with their limited knowledge of the English language. He learned to love the country that gave him refuge, but to the end, he remained a man of Russian culture, a Russian poet. Boris Gankin is buried in Ann Arbor, Michigan.

CHAPTER 13

Uncle Zhenya

Evgeny Gankin

My father's only surviving brother was a very talented man. When he was three, he was already drawing with an amazing likeness. Since he grew up in a very orthodox family, it presented a problem. First, his father strongly disapproved of such talents. To him, drawing was a waste of time. Human image making of any kind was more than that; it was a serious sin.

Little Yevel, later known to the world as Evgeny, or just Uncle Zhenya to me, would hide under the table and draw the biblical faces of old men, the portraits of his many siblings, the kind face of his mom. His dad caught and punished him more than once, but that didn't stop him.

In 2021, my sister, Inessa Gankin, was conducting research for an article she was writing. She was browsing through the archives of Vitebsk and stumbled upon a letter written by my grandfather Afroim-Mordukh in 1930, as well as childhood drawings of his son, my dad's younger brother.

This is the note from the archives, in my translation: "On July 31, 1930, a resident of Shchedrin, Bobruisk district, Mordukh Gankin, sent a letter to the teachers of the Belarussian Art Union reporting that his 8-year-old son Yevel was drawing extremely well. In his native town, everyone admired the boy's drawings and believed that he had real talent. However, there were no teachers in Shchedrin who could teach Yevel, and his father asked Vitebsk specialists for advice. To prove his son's talent, Mordukh Gankin has attached several drawings of his son, which are now preserved in the State Archives of the Vitebsk region."

The letter is of a parent, proud of his eight-year-old son's drawings, asking the artists guild in the larger city of Vitebsk to help him find an art teacher for his talented son. Amazingly, it was written by the same man who objected to his son's talent in the beginning. Unbelievable, but somehow, ninety years later, this letter found us.

Another amazing thing: Among these drawings was a portrait of Leon Trotsky, proudly identifying the man in the portrait as such. Trotsky, the most influential man in the country after Lenin's death, lost a power struggle to Stalin. He was declared an enemy of the state and expelled from the Soviet Union in February of 1929. Though the mass arrests of his followers did not start until several years later, drawing and sending his portrait was a very dangerous move, even in 1930. Nevertheless, nothing bad happened to the family. The death machine was only getting ready for the mass purges.

Often, talented people are talented in more than one field. Yevel started writing poetry very early. His first language was Yiddish, and it naturally became the language of his juvenile poems. At that time, there were still multiple Yiddish publications in the Soviet Union and, of course, in Belarus where Yiddish was one of the four official languages.

Evgeny Gankin left a book of memoirs, which our family published in the United States after his death. It is a well-written book, with many interesting details noted with his artist's eye. One of the chapters begins with "I adored Izi Kharik."

Izi Kharik, a famous Yiddish poet, came to read his poetry in Shchedrin when Uncle Zhenya was only ten. He had been writing naive poems since first grade, but this visit inspired him, and he dedicated more and more time to his verses. His teacher sent the boy's best poem to Izi Kharik, and parts of it were published in the Yiddish magazine *Shtern*. The author was twelve.

I found out from my uncle's book that, at that time, my father wrote a letter to Izi Kharik who responded that Uncle Zhenya had a definite talent and must continue writing. After that, the aspiring poet sent all his poems directly to Kharik, always receiving responses with critique and encouragement. On his esteemed colleague's initiative, at age thirteen, Evgeny Gankin became a recipient of a special stipend (seventy-five rubles) as a promising gifted poet.

Izi Kharik was one of the best Yiddish poets of that time. He was born into a poor family in a small shtetl in Belarus. He accepted the Bolshevik Revolution and Communist ideology with great enthusiasm. As a volunteer, he fought in the Russian Civil War. He was not just a talented poet but also an innovator of the Yiddish language. He published numerous books of poetry. He held many important positions in the government and was a corresponding member of the Belarussian Academy of Sciences. His devotion to Communism did not save him. In 1937, he was arrested. Following his arrest, his wife was detained too. Their children were sent to an orphanage for "members of families of enemies of the people."

Now we know more details of his last months. He was arrested together with more than twenty people—all representatives of the Jewish creative intelligentsia. All of them were accused of anti-Soviet activities. First, he, like many others before and after him, naively believed that it was by mistake. Later, he was brutally tortured into confessing to crimes he did not commit. A broken man, he admitted and signed everything and named other people as his coconspirators. At night, dragged from interrogations, half-conscious, he screamed in Yiddish "*Far vos*?" (What did I do?" Why?)He was sentenced to death and executed on October 29, 1937. Izi Kharik was thirty-nine. His wife spent almost twenty years in the Gulag. When she came back, she never found her children. They disappeared without a trace.

My uncle was deeply affected by what happened to Izi Kharik. For him, the poet was a mentor, a man he strived to emulate. He sank into depression and, six months later, emerged from it with deep scars. He never wrote poetry again. At that time, he was fifteen and already lived with my parents.

Evgeny and Aron Gankin

My mom often joked that she married a man with a child. Uncle Zhenya was ten years younger than my dad. With all his talents, a seven-year school in a small shtetl was just not good enough for him. Immediately after my parents got married, he moved in with them.

I don't know where this trait of my parents came from. Was it common to all traditional families? Was it from my parents' religious upbringing? All I know is that both my parents treated each other's families as their own. Different requirements and double standards simply did not exist. My mom's sisters stayed with us, as did my dad's nieces and nephews. The only grandparent I knew, my maternal grandfather, lived with us for a long time, and my dad was thrilled with it. Often, married people use each other's relatives as weapons, sometimes with quite deadly consequences. For my parents, it was just not the case.

Gomel was no Paris, but it had decent nine-year schools and good teachers. Drawing and painting seemed safer to young Zhenya than writing, putting his thoughts into words.

After graduating, he was accepted by the State *Institute of Cinematography,* also known as VGIK, the most famous film school in Moscow—no small feat for a provincial boy. In 1941, when Nazi Germany attacked the Soviet Union, German troops were moving closer and closer to the capital. To assist the Red Army, divisions of the Moscow people's militia were formed.

My uncle was among the defenders of Moscow. Later, several of the most promising students were called away from the front and sent to the city of Alma-Ata in Kazakhstan to resume their studies.

Fortunately for my uncle, at that time, the famous director Sergei Eisenstein was filming his epic movie *Ivan the Terrible* at the Alma-Ata Studios. Eisenstein started giving him and several other hungry students some assignments, mostly to help them in their desperate situation. Later, probably noticing my then twenty-year-old uncle's talent, he made him the second artist in *Ivan the Terrible*—Stalin's effort to boost morale during the war.

In his book, Evgeny Gankin draws an interesting portrait of the famous filmmaker, whom he first met when he was seventeen. Eisenstein, already the world-renowned creator of *Battleship Potemkin, was then only forty.*

Uncle Zhenya had a very successful career in the movie industry, and was the recipient of many awards. He was the head of the Art Department at Belarusfilm, the main movie studio in Belarus.

Lidia Arabei, Evgeny Gankin

He married a talented Belarusian writer, Lidia Arabei. Although not Jewish, she became a full-fledged member of our very Jewish family, and my mom took good care of her when she was sick.

In our family album, there are pictures of Uncle Zhenya with Vladimir Vysotsky, Marina Vlady, Anatoly Rybakov, Vasil Bykov, and other Russian and Belarusian celebrities. He had a very interesting life. He was allowed to travel abroad, albeit only to Socialist countries, which

Evgeny Gankin, Vladimir Vysotsky

was still much more than most of his fellow Jews could do.

My uncle was a very reserved man. I was his youngest niece. I certainly was attached to him, and I believe he loved me, but we never spoke openly, as two adults. I have more questions than answers about him. Did he like his work? I think he did. Did he reach his potential? I believe he did not. Was he happy or content? I will never find out. Was he forever wounded by the death of his mentor? Was he ever able to overcome this trauma? I know that his non-Jewish wife was always more outspoken about anti-Semitism and the Soviet system than he was. Was he a little ashamed of his Jewishness? Was he a little embarrassed by his overtly Jewish brother and sister-in-law? All this is very possible. However, I know that he always remembered how my mom asked Dad during the hungry war years to send only half of his officer's salary to her and their son, with the other half going to his younger brother.

All I know is that both my parents treated *each other's families as their own.*

CHAPTER 14

Poor Raya

I am not sure why I remember the following episode so well. After all, at that time I was only three and a half. I think it was probably because I never saw adults crying before. I remember my mom explaining to me what happened, and I can still hear her voice.

I knew you'd ask me millions of questions about Aunt Raya. What do you want to know? Wow, you have only two questions. Lucky me! You only need to know why she was crying and why she spent the night here when she lives next door. Well, this is easier asked than answered.

You know Uncle Misha, her husband. They have been married for fifteen years, almost as long as your dad and I. They had a good marriage. He is not a drunk, and he loves her. He is not Jewish, but it never caused any problems before. They have two kids. Everything was fine until recently.

Unfortunately, Uncle Misha can read. No, no, knowing how to read is a good thing; I was just kidding. Reading is not the problem; the problem is what he reads. The newspapers are so full of hate and lies these days. Even a small child understands that doctors are treating people, not killing them, right? Well, I wish all adults had your brains. I don't know what's wrong with people these days. They believe that Jewish doctors are poisoning their patients left and right. A perfectly healthy man comes to visit his doctor and drops dead in ten minutes because this doctor's just killed him. Can you believe it?

Good God, even a small kid knows this is a bunch of lies. Well, where was I? Ah yes, we were talking about poor Aunt Raya. Her genius of a husband reads the newspaper and tells her, "Do you see what your Jews are doing?" Oh, no, he still loves her. He believes that his Raya is good; she is just different from all the other Jews. There is an old saying: "My own Chaim is not a Yid."

Do you know what the worst thing is? It's her older daughter who, by the way, is not a baby; she is fifteen and a regular cow in size. Yesterday, when Aunt Raya was speaking with me in Yiddish, I noticed that this girl was mocking her own mother behind her back. I will tell you, nothing is worse than when your own flesh and blood is ashamed of you. I love you to pieces, but I will kill you if I ever notice that you are ashamed of being Jewish. Be ashamed of bad Jews, but be proud of being Jewish.

Why is this kid crying again? Enough already. Of course, I am not going to kill you; it was just a figure of speech. Milk? Of course, no milk. Bread with butter? Sure, it's not Chanukah, not a time for miracles today. That's too bad! We are ready for a miracle; otherwise, only God knows where we all will be a month from now.

For those who are not familiar with the details, let me explain what was happening. In January of 1953, the leading Soviet newspaper *Pravda* published an article titled "Vicious Spies and Killers under the Mask of Academic Physicians." The majority of the doctors accused of being paid agents of Zionist organizations and of poisoning and attempting to kill top government officials were Jewish. They were arrested and brutally tortured in order to obtain their confessions.

The anti-Semitic propaganda campaign was getting increasingly vicious. Many Jews, including my parents, were expecting deportation to Siberia.

Unfortunately, it is well-known that only a small percentage of independently thinking people can resist massive propaganda. Stalin and Hitler both knew it and very successfully used misinformation to brainwash their people. *Stalin's* brilliant *propaganda machine* fooled even the most prominent Western intellectuals, people who had free access to information. Many of them flocked to Moscow and were absolutely charmed by the "great Stalin." Similar propaganda and hatred are running amok now, even at American campuses. Small wonder that for most Soviet people the content of the *Pravda* editorial was beyond any doubt.

My parents were neighbors with a married couple, Misha and Raya. As my mom explained, she was Jewish, and he was not. They had a good marriage. He was the sole provider for the family, and he loved his wife. They had two kids. Everything was fine until one day in the early fifties when, overwhelmed by propaganda, he told her that Jews were always traitors.

She cried on my mom's shoulder for a while, and then returned home to her husband. Their family survived; they did not divorce. She was a stay-at-home mom; she did not have too many options.

Poor Raya! Many times in my life in the Soviet Union, people told me that I was a surprisingly good person, not like all the other Jews. They did not even realize that they were insulting me. The expression "you are different from all the other Jews" was a cliché many of my Jewish friends heard from time to time. In the minds of these people, it was the biggest compliment to a Jew they could think of. Each time, I felt deeply wounded, but at least these people were strangers to me. Poor Raya!

I knew you'd ask me millions of questions about Aunt Raya.

What do you want to know?

CHAPTER 15

Maxim Isaakovich

I don't remember the evening of March 5, 1953, the day of Stalin's death. When I grew up, Mom told me about it many times, and I hope I can repeat her story word for word.

This man was crazy. Don't look at me like that! I know that Maxim Isaakovich was a good and very bright man, but to come to our door and say, "The cockroach kicked the bucket," when everyone knew what had just been announced on the radio! He was crazy; his previous arrest taught him nothing. To come here, to close the door, and to whisper— that I would understand, that would be normal. He could jump for joy all he wanted, but he chose to announce it at full volume in times like these, when all our neighbors were crying their eyes out for Stalin. Believe me, when he said it, your dad turned snow white too.

My first thought was "Will there be pogroms?" I was terrified. What will happen to our children? You were always sick. What if the rumors were true? How would we survive if all Jews were deported to Siberia? We have heard that in

*Moscow they were already preparing the railroad cars. You'd
never survive even the trip there, let alone life in Siberia.
During the war, we at least knew where to run. With this anti-
Semitic campaign, I was afraid that our own neighbors would
start killing us any day.*

*In addition, maybe I was crazy, but I was still a bit sorry
that Stalin died. Don't look at me like that; after all, we
fought the war with his name. My father called Stalin Haman,
like in the Purim story, and my father was always right, but
still, I was so confused.*

My mom was not the only one who was confused that night.
It seems incredible that in a country devastated by Stalin's
purges, in a country where millions of people died of starvation
because of these purges and his agricultural policy, so many
people attended his funeral that many were trampled to death
in the crowd crush.

I remember very well the huge monument to Stalin, which
dominated the Central Square of Minsk. It survived Stalin by
nine years and disappeared only in 1962, in the Khrushchev era,
toppled by two tanks in the middle of the night.

I also remember the life story of our neighbor, Maxim
Isaakovich, as told by my mom. It is worth remembering
because he was one of the few people who fully understood,
even at that time, the horror and pain that Stalin and his regime
inflicted on the Soviet people.

A talented boy born to poor parents, he was betrothed to a
plain rich girl, whose parents agreed to educate him abroad. He
studied in Paris and London and became a very accomplished
engineer. He fulfilled his promises, returned to Russia, and
married this girl. Together, they had a daughter, Sonia, and they
spoiled her silly.

After the Bolshevik Revolution, he continued to do what he did best—work as a mechanical engineer. The Cheka, the Soviet Secret Police of that time, confiscated all their money. In 1938, during the mass campaign against "spies and saboteurs," Maxim Isaakovich was arrested and accused of being a German spy. Most of those arrested were tortured into confessions.

Keeping his head cool even under torture, Maxim Isaakovich told these monsters that he would never sign a confession on espionage or sabotage charges. He offered to confess to being a thief. Since the goal was to put him in prison, the interrogator agreed. Instead of getting a life sentence or being executed as a spy, he got away with "only" five years in prison for larceny.

Being a "common criminal" saved his life during the first days of the war. As the Germans were approaching Minsk, all the prisoners were separated into two groups. The political prisoners were shot, and the common criminals were let go. He escaped Minsk on foot and made it to the Soviet lines. His wife was killed in the Minsk ghetto. His daughter Sonia, a musician, was on a tour as an accompanist when the war started. She survived.

He returned to Minsk in 1947 but was only fully exonerated in 1956. When we moved into the next room, he befriended our family. His unmarried daughter sometimes brought men home, sending her father away for several hours. He, like so many others, found shelter in our small room. He spoke many languages fluently and helped my brother with his French lessons. He had a wonderful library, lent his books to the capable boy Boris, and strongly influenced him. A strident anti-Stalinist, he, to my mom's horror, openly and loudly discussed his views with my father.

I was too little to interest him. His only phrase related to me became a family legend. Once, at the age of two, I was throwing a tantrum for no good reason, when he told my mom, "Be careful, or she'll grow up to be a spoiled brat, just like my Sonia."

I did not have time to disprove it; I had not seen him since I was seven. I remember him as old and shrunken but never broken. This chapter is my modest tribute to this freethinking man.

Being a "common criminal" saved his life *during the first days of the war.*

CHAPTER 16

Efim Pavlovich

One day, Mom happily
announced that we were going
to have a wedding in the family.

*Roza and Efim Pavlovich
(Chaim Faivelevich) Kabak*

*A wedding is always such a
happy event. My sister Roza,
your aunt, will finally have a
family. She had a fiancé many
years ago, but he perished
in the war. She has a good
figure and excellent legs, but
it's so difficult for a woman
to marry these days. Most of
the suitable men fought in
the war, so few came back
home. They say that there are seven women for every man
of marriageable age. I don't know where this one man may
be, but it seems that he is always either married or drunk
all the time.*

The war is over, but there's still so much grief and sadness hanging in the air. I don't even remember the last time I was at a wedding. It's time to live a little, I guess. Of course, I will cook for the wedding. Who else is going to do it? It doesn't mean that I cannot look smart. What do you think? I can buy a new lace collar. They are not that expensive. Maybe Dad and I can dance a little. Forty-one is not that old; we are still young. Wedding! They may even have kids. You will have little cousins. I am so excited! After all these tears, and deaths, we will have a wedding, one more wedding in the family!

This is how I first heard about Efim Kabak, my uncle Efim, who became a very important part of my life. He was originally from Poland and grew up in a wealthy family in Warsaw. He traveled the world in his youth, mostly on his bicycle. Twice he visited Palestine with the goal of staying there, and twice he returned to Warsaw. When he was already very ill, he said that coming back to Poland was the biggest mistake of his life. His entire family—his parents, his sisters, his first wife, his daughter, and his granddaughter—was killed by the Nazis.

He was a man of considerable literary talent, but in his young years, he believed that everyone should be exposed to manual labor. His family was too bourgeois for him. His parents wanted him to become a doctor or a lawyer, but according to his memoirs, he believed in his youth that "all doctors are charlatans and all lawyers are crooks." He tried different occupations—worked on a farm, was a security guard in a kibbutz, but ended up with a very unromantic job. He became an accountant in the Soviet Union. He fathered his first daughter out of wedlock, but in his memoirs, he warned his second daughter not to be too trustful of men. Life is so ironic sometimes.

In the gray monotony of postwar Soviet life, he was like an exotic bird from a tropical paradise. He was a free man, a man who had seen the world. His native language was Polish, but he had graduated from a Russian gymnasium, and his Russian was perfect. He knew many languages, and on his bookshelves, beside volumes in Polish and Russian, there were books in other languages too. Brilliant and artistic, he was a fantastic storyteller. He was the first person I saw performing skits at parties. He would put on my mom's dressing gown and a kerchief, move his chin forward in a certain way, and, by some magic, would look exactly like an old *bubbe* (grandma) from a shtetl. I don't remember his exact words, but I do remember my dad laughing so hard that tears streamed down his cheeks.

With my uncle Efim Kabak

Despite having many reasons to dislike his native land, he passionately loved Poland and the Polish language. He taught me to read in Polish. At a time when finding good books in Russian was very difficult, I used my knowledge of Polish to read *The Diary of Anne Frank* and many other books I couldn't buy in Russian.

Being as poor as or poorer than everyone else, he could live without necessities but not without the extras. He would take a taxi to go to the theater and order a glass of champagne for his wife, even if it meant they both would have a meager dinner tomorrow. He was extremely hot-tempered and always discussed politics with my father very frankly and very loudly, making Mom draw the curtains and check every five minutes if someone was eavesdropping at the door.

In Minsk, he worked as the chief accountant at the Belarusian Theater of Opera and Ballet. He fit in very well there, and even the spoiled prima donnas were able to find many things in common with him and liked him a lot. As a fringe benefit, he always got free passes to the best performances, and willingly shared them with me. Though my parents took me to this theater for the first time when I was three, I credit my real love of opera to my school days, when I was at the Opera Theater much more frequently than my parents would have been able to afford without Uncle Efim's help.

As my mom hoped, Efim and Roza had a child, my talented sister Inna, who was born in 1958. After Innochka was born, her mom became sick, and then very sick. She died in 1965, but little Inna mostly stayed with us even before her death. Efim Pavlovich was in our apartment almost every working day; my parents loved him and he loved them back. Innochka spent the weekends and vacations with him. I am sure he was much more fun than my strict mom and quiet dad.

With Inessa Gankin and her husband, Dmitry Simonov

He fought cancer for many years, and showed unusual courage, patience, and incredible optimism, even when there was no hope left. In times of gloom, he always had a smile and a joke for everyone.

He died in 1968, and later, Innochka was adopted by my parents. It was her wish, and they were very happy with it. They loved her, worried about her, and tried to protect her in any way they could.

Inessa Gankin is a psychologist, a teacher, and, most of all, a very talented poet and writer. She inherited her father's free spirit and often speaks her mind. She is a public figure in Belarus, but to me she will always be the cute little girl with whom I shared a bedroom until I was eighteen.

Despite having many reasons to dislike his native land,

he passionately loved Poland and the Polish language.

CHAPTER 17

The New Apartment

Sarah and Hanan Zunz

In Mikhail Bulgakov's book *The Master and Margarita,*
Woland (Satan), observing the behavior of the Muscovites,
notes that the housing problem has corrupted their
characters. This was true not only of the Muscovites. The
shortage of housing created many phenomena, among them
communal apartments.

My uncle Honya in Leningrad shared a kitchen with six
other families. His own family (himself, his wife, and their four
children) occupied two small rooms. Seven families sharing
the kitchen, seven women cooking, seven kerosene stoves, God
knows how many people sharing the same toilet, a multitude of
kids screaming day and night—a little communal hell. Besides,
he was the only sibling of my mom's who strictly observed
Jewish law all his life, including kashrut (Jewish dietary laws).
His family had to do it under these conditions.

We shared our kitchen with only one neighbor, but the
living conditions were still very bad. During the war, Minsk
was almost completely destroyed. I remember the high fences
behind which the new buildings were being built. Most avenues
and streets in the city, which is over a thousand years old, are
younger than I am.

My first memories of Minsk are full of curvy narrow streets
with small wooden houses. This was the area of the ghetto,
which by some miracle had survived the bombardments and
fires. During the cold winter months, I could see the Christmas
ornaments and bright confetti placed on cotton wool between
my neighbors' window frames. I remember huge snowdrifts;
they were much taller than I was then. The snowdrifts were
white after the snowfall, but quickly became grayer and grayer. I
also recall the smell of burning wood and the sound of dry snow
squeaking under my little white felt boots. My first winters were
like old engravings—black-and-white.

During the summer, I remember playing with my friend in a tiny front garden beneath the windows of their apartment. Besides having a small garden, their apartment had many other advantages: It was a single-family unit, with two big sunny rooms and a modern bathroom—very luxurious when compared with our communal one.

My friend was a plump girl, six months older and a full head shorter than I was. She really liked her food, and my mom was always lecturing me on how some women were lucky to have a daughter with a good appetite.

Mom, Manya, and me

While my only toy was Manya, a celluloid doll whose chic wardrobe consisted of one dress made by my mom, my friend had a big colorful ball, several dolls dressed in bright dresses, and even the ultimate luxury—a miniature porcelain tea set for teatime with her dolls. They always had some hard-to-buy food in their home: bright orange mandarins in the winter, hothouse cucumbers in the spring. Food never made me jealous. Toys possibly did.

Many years later, I found out that her dad, an imperceptible little man, was known among his colleagues by the tender name of "phial of poison." He was an auditor, and especially liked auditing grocery stores. In times when food was scarce, he would bring home bags full of provisions. He did not disdain money either.

The housing problem certainly did not improve his

personality. At that time, apartments were distributed to people; one could not just go and buy them. When my parents were about to finally get a new one-bedroom apartment with all the modern conveniences, my best friend's dad signaled to the authorities that our current living conditions did not justify us getting a new place to live. It cost my parents a lot of grief. When confronted by another neighbor, he gave the following explanation: "My wife told me that she would die if the Gankins got a new apartment and we didn't."

Looking back, I am very glad that I grew up without that tiny tea set, the dream of my childhood, but with my honest and decent parents.

With my parents

CHAPTER 18

Our Neighbors From Argentina

Of all the neighbors who shared a kitchen with us or lived nearby, one family really stood out. They had very simple Slavic names: Piotr Antonovich and Matryona Ignatievna. He was a big and attractive man, while she was a small, quiet, mousy woman with a kind smile who wore her hair in a tight bun. She was always totally overshadowed by her strong, tough husband. All their three children spoke Russian with a slight accent. They also moved with an unusual grace of dancers, something not very common in the Soviet Union at that time.

Eventually, this family became friends with ours, and I, listening silently close to my mom's knee, learned their life story.

Piotr Antonovich and Matryona Ignatievna were born in Western Belarus, which before 1939 was part of Poland. She was the daughter of a well-off farmer; he was a hired hand at their farm. I don't know for sure if it was a marriage of love or convenience on his side. Anyway, they married for life, and eventually had three children in the family. They both loved their land and worked hard on it. In 1939, it became obvious that Soviet occupation was imminent. Fearing the worst, they sold their land and moved to Argentina. They made a good life there. Spanish became the language of their children.

Everything was great, except Piotr Antonovich suffered from a bad case of nostalgia. He listened to radio programs from the Soviet Union and became more and more influenced by their very effective propaganda. He became a member of the Communist Party of Argentina. Listening every day to the blatant lies about the wonderful lives of the peasants and workers in the USSR, he decided that it was time to bring his children back to his homeland.

They arrived in his beloved Belarus with the first group of repatriates from Argentina. They were very lucky—it was 1955, and Stalin was already dead. Only two years earlier, the authorities would have sent them directly to Siberia to perish in the Gulag. Now, they received a room in a wooden barrack, and then, a year later, a one-bedroom flat in a big apartment building next door to us.

Piotr Antonovich quickly realized that he had made a horrible mistake. Soon after arriving, he burned his Communist Party membership card. That was easy. Much harder was facing his children who blamed him for bringing them to the totalitarian country.

One of his first thoughts was to prevent his friends still in Argentina from making the same mistake. At that time, phone calls abroad were unheard of. The letters would certainly be opened and inspected by the KGB censors. Then he had a bright idea. He wrote to Argentina about the great life in the Soviet Union, freedom and equality for all. He suggested they follow in his steps as soon as possible. He then recommended a store in Buenos Aires as the only place where they could buy all they would ever need in the USSR.

The letter was most likely opened and deemed harmless. The recipients of the letter decided to stay in Argentina. Piotr Antonovich had named a funeral home as the only place to buy stuff for their happy return to the Soviet Union.

My parents were very sympathetic to their plight and always spoke openly about their problems. I remember Piotr Antonovich explaining to Dad that in Argentina, my dad, with his education and skills, would own a big villa. Dad was smiling his unassuming smile; villas were very far from his thoughts. I also remember Mom sending a plate of matzah to them on Passover and receiving painted eggs in return on Easter. My parents, though staunchly Jewish, were always open to good people of any religion around them.

I followed the life of this family for many years. The only "lucky" person who was able to escape her father's homeland was their daughter, who contracted tuberculosis and was let go for humanitarian reasons. The family was separated forever. Their elegant sons lost the lightness in their stride and learned to keep their thoughts to themselves. The younger son discovered alcohol. Many years later, the strong-willed man Piotr Antonovich committed suicide.

CHAPTER 19

Books

Even in the most difficult times, parents try to shield their children from the harsh reality by creating a warm home for them. My childhood was no exception. If ever love could protect a child, my parents' love was certainly sheltering me, sometimes too much. Eventually, though, the child grows up, goes to school, meets other people, and the outside world is not always kind to them.

I was lucky—being a quiet kid and an excellent student helped me thrive in school. For good or bad, I was loved by most teachers, genuinely liked studying, and was always bored after a couple of weeks of summer break. I had many pals, but my most intimate friends, my soul mates, were books.

I learned to read on my fourth birthday. As a gift, Uncle Zhenya and Aunt Lida had brought me small wooden alphabet cubes. My mom proclaimed that I was too young to study the alphabet, but they showed me the letters anyway, and the next day I was reading, first slowly, then quickly, and soon very, very quickly.

In my parents' home, there were always books, even in times when buying them meant going on without something else, sometimes quite important. A well-known slogan proclaimed "a book is the best gift," and my parents believed in it. Both my brother and I received books for good grades, for good behavior, as birthday or New Year presents, or just because. Our small apartment had the complete works of Tolstoy and Pushkin, Balzac and Dickens, Dostoevsky and Ehrenburg— volumes and volumes of books. I already mentioned that we also had the complete works of Marx and Lenin, which my dad was obligated to buy, but I am sure that no one in the family ever opened them.

Nobody controlled my choice of literature. Food was a different story. It was my mom's domain, and she didn't give me any choice at all, either with selection or with quantity. The refrain of my childhood was "Swallow! Chew and swallow; chew and swallow. Look into this mirror at your left cheek. It's twice as big as your right one. It's no longer bread; it is a cud, a camel's cud. Will you swallow it today, or should we wait until tomorrow for this miracle to happen? Chew and swallow, chew and swallow." For a woman who knew real hunger and made heroic efforts to feed her child during the war, food was the best gift she could give her loved ones. It was characteristic not only of my mom. Whenever guests knocked on the door, whether they announced their arrival in advance or not, there was always food on the table.

I always joke that I married young to escape force-feeding. It is funny, but only then did I learn to enjoy my food. Before that, I was dreaming of a glorious future when, instead of eating, people would be able to just swallow a pill and be done with it. When Mom stopped controlling my food intake, little by little, I realized that there were things I actually liked. I stopped keeping food behind my cheeks. Because of how my mom raised me, I never forced my kids to eat. I still hate boiled milk and cream of wheat, though.

With books, everything was different. They were right there, very accessible, and I read many classical works of literature before the age of full comprehension. Whenever I was sick, and I was sick very often, books entertained me and kept me company.

Since that time, I have learned to create little stories in my head. At five, in some of these stories I was a beautiful princess—at sixteen, a very attractive girl with whom a real prince was in love. The stories, as one can see, did not change much, though the dialogues became more elaborate and the main female protagonist more sophisticated. In reality, I was very shy and not self-confident, and even in my romantic imagination, I was mostly reserved and unattainable.

I don't remember exactly when I discovered poetry. I know that I have rhymed since I was three, but by discovering poetry, I mean the real thing—Pushkin, Tyutchev, Tsvetaeva, and so many others. I remember that by the age of fourteen, I knew whole chapters from *Eugene Onegin* and hundreds of poems by heart, and they deeply touched me. I still remember most of them, and in the most difficult moments of my life, I can always bring beauty into my collapsing world.

At fourteen, I, like many other children from good families before and after me, was writing poems—poems about love and life, war and death—deeply emotional and romantic poems of a fourteen-year-old. I don't remember who noticed my verses, but they were published in local newspapers, and at sixteen, I was a frequent guest on Belarusian TV and radio. I read my poems while the light projectors in the TV studio were frying both my face and my brain. One professional composer even wrote music to one of my poems (about love and life, of course), and I received hundreds of fan letters, many of which opened with the same phrase: "In the first lines of my letter . . ."

What really bothers me is that I cannot look at my poems now to see if I had any real talent. By eighteen, I decided to quit poetry forever and destroyed all my writings. Partially, this decision was influenced by my brother's desperate attempts to be published. I just didn't want to go this route. The very few that survived the purges met the same fate twenty years later, when we were emigrating. The Soviet government did not allow traitors to take any manuscripts with them. I will write more about that later.

Though I very seldom write verses anymore, the world possibly lost a decent poet, but it certainly did not lose a reader, a devotee, and an enthusiast of poetry.

My love of literature is probably the most comfortable, most sheltered part of my life. In some sense, it is a sublimation of reality, which is often difficult and unfair. Life is rarely tranquil in general, and my life certainly is not an exception. Nevertheless, in the most difficult times, my internal, imaginary world is with me, as beautiful and peaceful as I want it to be.

I still remember most of them, and in the most difficult moments of my life, *I can always bring beauty into my collapsing world.*

CHAPTER 20

A Train To Gomel

The real, external world was different. I could not always wave a magic wand of my imagination and make everything just and fair. I forgot many things, but I think I can pinpoint the moment when I first understood why my parents always pronounced the word *Jewish* in a soft voice, almost in a whisper.

In 1956, my mom and I embarked on our yearly summer journey to Gomel to visit my grandfather. I remember this trip very well—the smell of coal, the stifling heat, the hot dark-red tea in clear glasses. At one moment, my mom exited our compartment, probably to go to the restroom, and left me alone with two middle-aged men in dark suits, hotly discussing world politics. I remember the bottle on the table and the nauseating smell of sausage and hard-boiled eggs, the usual fare of travelers.

A day earlier, Egypt had nationalized the Suez Canal, and newspapers were talking about a potential war with Israel. I knew very little about either Israel or the war, but I knew the word *Jewish* very well. I will never forget their words: "Jews will be fighting! Ha, ha! I would like to see their rifles. They are probably as crooked as their noses," said one. "They didn't fight in the war because they were cowards. They all ran off to Tashkent to hide," agreed the second man, thoughtfully chewing the sausage.

I wanted to tell them, "My dad is Jewish, and he fought in the war. My uncles fought, and one of them was killed fighting." I was seven; I never uttered a word. I also never forgot that trip. The humiliation and shame of it are with me even today, many years later.

When I grew older, little by little I learned to speak my mind. It was and still is very hard for me to confront people, but it is even harder to suffer the indignity of not responding. I did not look typically Jewish and often overheard similar rants while standing in lines to buy food, while traveling, or even at work. I quickly learned that even a quiet rebuke often brought apologies and even more often an immediate response that my opponent had a Jewish friend, boss, or neighbor with whom he or she, of course, was on the best of terms. I recently watched *Gentlemen's Agreement*, a fine movie about anti-Semitism in America in the forties, and the line "Some of your best friends are Methodists, too, but you never seem to mention that" made me laugh. I guess anti-Semites are the same everywhere.

Deep inside me, there is still this little girl who kept silent that day. I have struggled with her all my life. I hope I am finally winning this fight.

CHAPTER 21

My First School Day

My first school day started
unremarkably. I remember
my brand-new school
uniform, a brown dress with
a white frilled pinafore-style
apron in front. On regular
days, a simpler black apron
would replace the white
one. This dress had a lacy
white collar which could be
easily detached and washed
separately. Similar cuffs

School uniform

adorned the sleeves. Handmade pom-poms, the pride of my
mom, decorated white knee-highs on my legs. The last detail
of this gorgeous outfit was a huge white hair bow, placed by
my mom on top of my unruly curly hair. I felt very grown-up
and refined.

This picture was taken later. In it, I am already a member of the Young Pioneers (an organization for children ages nine to fourteen that operated between 1922 and 1991 and wear a red scarf, but it gives the reader an idea of our uniform.)

I remember a big, heavy bunch of red gladioli in one of my hands and a brand-new schoolbag in the other. All the first graders were standing together in the schoolyard, in front of the rest of the students. Proud moms were wiping their eyes and blowing their noses. I noticed that I was the tallest one and really disliked this fact. My instinctive desire was to blend in with the crowd.

The parents went home, and the teachers took the children into their classrooms and told each of them where to sit. Our teacher was dressed in a navy blue woolen dress and wore her graying hair in a bun over a wrinkled face. She assigned two students to each wooden desk. The desks were old, scratched by the pocketknives of those who sat there before us. A large blackboard hung on the wall. Our teacher lectured us about discipline in school. She concentrated on forbidden activities, and never mentioned the permitted ones. I did not feel grown-up and sophisticated anymore. Then she opened a class register and read our names, adding "nationality" to each of them.

To people in the United States, *Jewish* means religion, but in the Soviet Union, it meant ethnicity. My American friends are usually very surprised to learn that people in the Soviet Union were obligated to state their ethnicity when opening a library account, checking into a hospital, just about everywhere. People of mixed ethnicity had a choice between their parents' ethnicities or, as they were called, nationalities. In the complicated hierarchy of multiple nationalities in the Soviet Union, one was at the very, very bottom. There was a joke that the answer to the question about one's nationality could be binary, either "Yes" or "No."

If only one of the parents was Jewish, the choice was clear—anything was better than being Jewish. The majority of people who stayed Jewish had no choice.

In this patriarchal society, children always took the last names of their fathers, with one notable exception: When the father was Jewish, and the mother wasn't, children often took their mother's last name. One of the more famous examples would be the former world chess champion Garry Kasparov who was born Garry Weinstein and adopted his mother's Armenian last name at the age of twelve.

As the teacher read our names, she asked each of us to stand up and answer a simple question. I don't remember the question she asked me, but I do remember a small and very scared boy whose answer to the question "How many legs does a cat have?" was "Eight." For the rest of the school year, his name was Sasha the Eight-Legged Cat.

The day is memorable to me, but not because of this funny episode. What happened to me then was a minor miracle. As a kid, I was unable to pronounce the rolled Russian *r* sound properly, which was considered a very Jewish trait. All of my mom's efforts to correct this problem were fruitless, and my mom was nothing if not a very determined person.

My *r* was soft, so most people didn't notice it right away. In my class, there was a Jewish girl, whose *r* was a very stereotypically Jewish guttural *rrr*. Unfortunately, this letter was present in her last name, and when she pronounced it, the eyes of my classmates sparkled. During recess, several boys and girls followed her, making the most exaggerated Jewish *RRR* sound and speaking with an overstated Jewish accent. I was terrified. I knew I would be next. Fear is a great motivator, and I came home from school pronouncing the sound *r* perfectly. At least in this aspect, starting from that day, I blended well.

CHAPTER 22

The School Years

As we get older and look back, most of us feel nostalgia for the past, for the times when we were young. I am always skeptical when people say that in their time everything was better. Some things were probably better; many others were worse. Society evolves, norms alter, people change, and there is only one truth in these statements—in our time, we were young and healthy, and life smiles on young and healthy people.

With that said, I still believe that my school years, starting from second grade, were happy. I was very lucky; I had good teachers and I was an able student, and good teachers usually like good students. The Soviet educational system was very tough on those who were not studious or talented enough to get good grades, and especially on those who were not willing to abide by the rules. Neither of the above applied to me. I was always ready for school, was well-behaved—perhaps even too well-behaved—and all subjects except for physical education were very easy for me.

My mom never had to do my homework with me. She trusted me, and I always trusted my kids to do their best, only helping them when asked.

Education in the Soviet Union was free and mandatory for everyone. Private or religious schools did not exist. Students were assigned to a certain school depending on where they lived. Fortunately, our apartment building, into which we moved before my second grade, was assigned to a school that soon became the best in our city.

From the first days of classes, we were sent home with a lot of homework. Besides the regular subjects, such as Russian language and arithmetic, in the first grade we also studied penmanship, one of my least favorite subjects. I was writing lines, hooks, and ovals for hours, until the lines were perfectly straight, the ovals were flawlessly oval, and the hooks were shaped ideally.

My mom was a great motivator; when I once brought home an imperfect grade (one of the hooks was a little flawed), I got a long lecture. At seven, it was difficult to comprehend all the horrible consequences of a defective hook. She told me that I would never enter a good university, would stay uneducated, and would be a disgrace to our family. She was not alone in this. There was a common understanding that, in order to succeed in life, Jews had to work harder than their non-Jewish classmates and needed better grades than other kids.

Mom scared me for life. Fortunately, imperfect hooks became less important with time, and I excelled easily in all other subjects. Since grades were always public knowledge, and many teachers never thought twice about humiliating bad students in front of the whole class and their poor parents in front of all the other parents, it was very fortunate not only for me but for my parents too.

Strictly academically, the school gave us a lot of knowledge. We memorized long poems by heart. In upper grades, we had special labs at school for physics and chemistry. We studied algebra, geometry, and trigonometry—not only by memorizing facts but also by proving the theorems and thus developing logical abilities. Our curriculum was compulsory; there were no electives.

Our marks went from one to five, with five being the highest. There was no grade curve. A whole grade could be deducted for a single misplaced comma in a lengthy composition or a minor error in a difficult math test. We got perfect grades for perfect work, period. Even bad handwriting or an inkblot could mean a lost grade.

Life proved my mom was right, possibly not in the choice of words but in essence. Perfect grades and great achievements at school were not always sufficient, but they certainly were necessary for entering a good university.

I very seldom received a grade that was not perfect and graduated from high school with a gold medal, the highest honor possible. I sometimes joke that the purpose of all this was to intimidate my future children with my achievements. Later, I married a man who was also a straight-A student both at school and at the university. It was very amusing for me to overhear one conversation between our daughters. It turned out that they envied their friends with, quoting them, "normal" parents who were not genuinely surprised by the occasional less than perfect grades of their children.

The school years were probably the happiest time of my life, so full of promises, of hopes, of friendships, of joie de vivre. I am grateful to my classmates for sharing these years with me.

CHAPTER 23

My Classmates

In parallel with the academic school life, there was a normal life, first of being a child, then of being a teenager, with its small joys and heartaches, friendships and quarrels, first disappointments and first romances. This life, day in and day out, was shared by my classmates.

My class still holds regular reunions. Every five years, my husband and I fly to Minsk to meet with my classmates. There are fewer and fewer people at our gatherings, but we are still there, and our meetings are full of warmth.

The last exams and the prom happened more than fifty years ago. I still keep in touch with some of my classmates. With many of them, I studied for ten years. Some of my old schoolmates are not with us anymore. There were those whom I judged shallow and not interesting, only to discover many years later that I was very wrong. Many of them were an important part of my childhood.

I am not going to paint here the portraits of all my schoolmates. I will talk only about those whose stories I find interesting or typical, or those who were or later became important to me.

A quiet boy, very undistinguished academically, usually sat in the back of the classroom. I never conversed with him one-on-one, barely knew his voice. During my school years, I did not know the most important thing about him—he was the son of a KGB colonel. Later, he followed in his dad's footsteps and went to work for the KGB right after college. At one of our reunions, I met a new man. This new man was not just self-confident; he was arrogant and offensive. He firmly positioned himself at the head of the table and started dishing out the truth about everyone. He told us that the time had come to arrange a car accident for one of our classmates who immigrated to Israel and was very active there. He knew that the Jewish husband of one of my classmates, a talented journalist, had received a prize in Poland, and he accused him of selling out to foreigners. He didn't know that my family already had invitations to Israel (most likely, he worked in a different city district); otherwise, I would definitely have gotten my share of verbal abuse. His tone was unbelievable. "Shut up, nobody asked for your opinion," he told one of our classmates. In the end, totally drunk, he announced that he was going to spend this night with one of our classmates. Since she had different plans, our men had to escort her home.

His drinking became such a huge problem that he was kicked out of the KGB, and died relatively young. After this reunion, I never saw him again, though I saw a picture from one of the later reunions, where he was conversing peaceably with the very same man whose death he had threatened to arrange.

Fortunately, the KGB didn't kill that man. I completely lost touch with him, and almost forty years later he contacted me on the Internet; since then, we have met many times in Israel, Minsk, and Ann Arbor. He showed his country to me with the pride of someone who has fought for it and built it. He loves it so passionately that even this alone makes me respect him. During these visits and from our correspondence, I found out many things about him that I didn't know at school.

While still very young, he became a Jewish activist. He was fighting for the rights of Jewish people to immigrate to Israel. He learned Hebrew and started teaching it, which in itself was a crime. All his activities were extremely dangerous in the Soviet Union and, though we were living in relatively "vegetarian" times, when people were not killed left and right as during Stalin's purges, Jewish activists were still going to prisons and labor camps for a lot less. He was involved with the distribution of samizdat, a very important form of dissident activity in the USSR, when people reproduced uncensored publications by hand or on a typewriter and spread them among sympathizers. Miraculously, he was able to immigrate to Israel in his early twenties. Though always very interested in history, he decided that he would be more useful to his country in a different capacity. He became a civil engineer and built many buildings, roads, and bridges in Israel. He seems to be in a very good place—a happy man, a suntanned and proud Israeli.

In the above paragraph, I used the term "vegetarian" times, which needs to be explained to the reader. The term "vegetarian years" was coined by a famous Russian poet, Anna Akhmatova. She referred to the post-Stalin times, when she and many other writers' voices were silenced, and their works were not published, as opposed to the years during Stalin's reign, where many talented writers, poets, and millions of less-known people were killed or "cannibalized."

Another classmate of mine also became a patriot of Israel, albeit a very unlikely one. Her mother worked as a janitor in our apartment building and was notorious for her anti-Semitism. My classmate later had two husbands, both heavy drinkers.

After two failed marriages, she raised her daughter alone. The daughter married a Jew and immigrated to Israel. My classmate visited her daughter many times, then finally married an Israeli and also moved to Israel. I was very impressed when she told me, "I am telling them [the Russian Jews] that if they live in Israel, they have to study Hebrew. I will never let anyone criticize Israel." I am very happy for her. For the first time in her life, she is content.

At our last class reunion, she took me aside and reminded me of a totally forgotten episode. She told me that many years ago she used an anti-Semitic slur in my presence. It was not directed at me, but I told her, "I am also Jewish." My classmate remembered this episode, thought about it for many years, and finally decided to take it off her chest and apologize to me. Her apologies were sincerely accepted, and I wish her all the best in her new Jewish life. I was actually proud to hear that at eight or nine I already knew that I had to reply and defend my ethnicity and my dignity.

Another one of my classmates was a very promising poet. He was also a very unpleasant boy, who started drinking very early in his life. Among his often-vulgar verses, there were lines of striking purity and lyricism. His father was in the military. His mom was the typical wife of a high-ranking army officer. She was well-dressed, well-cared for, didn't work, and had only one son. At a certain point, the girls in our class got tired of his drinking and constant harassment, which was very sexual even in eighth grade. A delegation went to see his mom. I was not a spokesperson, but I was present, in their large and nicely furnished (by Soviet standards) apartment. My classmate's mom told us that we were making it all up, that her son would never do anything like this, and she showed us the door. That day, God gave her the chance to change her son's life, but she didn't use it. Her talented son grew up only to become an alcoholic and die very young.

My best friend Valya came to our school in eighth grade. I don't remember which of us decided that we should become friends. Most likely, knowing our personalities, it was Valya, and I am very glad that she did it.

Valya

Valya lived far from our school and from the city center, and whenever we had any after-school projects or some interesting plans for the evening, she stayed with us, in our apartment. We had the same friends, did the same extracurricular activities, and often went together to our Opera and Ballet Theater. People frequently called us sisters, since we both had dark hair and dark eyes and were as thin as sticks. Valya liked my family, and I knew very well her kind mom and her sister and really liked them. My mom was always trying to feed her, and Valya always called her Auntie Rivochka, using the endearment form of my mom's name Riva.

I didn't realize it then, but Valya was a much stronger person than I was at that time. A young woman, right after university, she went to work in Kamchatka, the most remote corner of the USSR. There she met her husband—a bright, intelligent, freethinking man, and together they had two sons. Valya first became a PhD, then a doctor of sciences, and finally a provost of a large university in Petropavlovsk-Kamchatsky.

When, after many years of not seeing each other, she and her husband came to visit us in the United States and we met, it felt like we never were separated, either by time or by distance. I was very proud of all her successes and of what kind of person "my sister" had become. Her premature death left a big hole in my heart.

Boris and I are very good friends with her wonderful husband Rem. We visited Kamchatka after Valya's death, and one of the moments which touched me the most might surprise my readers. Rem and Andrei, Valya's older son, were seeing us off to the airport. We said our goodbyes, and when I turned to wave at them for the last time, I saw that Andrei, who is a devout Russian Orthodox Christian, was crossing our backs, wishing us a safe trip. My Jewishness was never a problem for Valya and her family. They liked me, and all my family loved Valya. I was so happy to see that their son inherited this from his parents, and us being Jewish didn't make him detest us. That is how it should be in an ideal world, but my world was rarely ideal, and that's why Andrei's gesture touched me so much.

CHAPTER 24

My Teachers

In the sixties, it became customary to create in every big city several schools with specialization in certain subjects. There were two most common types of specialized schools: physics/mathematics schools and schools with advanced study of a foreign language. These schools were prestigious, and they admitted students from other school districts too. My school became a physics/mathematics school, where both these subjects were taught at a higher level.

The physics teacher was not very much to write home about, but, starting from the eighth grade, I had a teacher of mathematics who was outstanding. He was a young man in his mid-twenties, and his methods of teaching were very unorthodox. First, he proved to us that we knew nothing. Nearly everyone flunked the initial tests he gave us. Then the real teaching began. We had tests where we were supposed to answer all questions while looking at a sandglass, which gave us only three minutes. It taught us not only to give the correct answers but also to formulate our thoughts in a precise and concise manner. Besides acquiring skills, we developed our logical abilities, the abilities to think and speak clearly.

The homework became increasingly challenging, not only by the sheer volume, but also by the difficulty of the problems we had to solve. We studied using not regular textbooks but much more complicated books, and the problems were often tricky. Many kids left our school to become good students elsewhere. Those who stayed later passed the mathematical entry exams at universities with flying colors.

Until eighth grade, I was thinking about a career in journalism. I changed my mind because of several factors. The first and the most important one was a conversation with my dad. One summer day, he took me aside, and in his quiet, mild manner told me that in the Soviet Union I would never be free to write what I wanted. The Communist Party or, even worse, the KGB would always control my writing. His unexpected bluntness made an impression, and I became more open-minded about my future career.

Several other things made me switch my interest from journalism to mathematics. One of them was my success at the Mathematical Olympiads. This was a time when all kinds of Olympiads for schoolchildren were very popular. We had Olympiads in math, physics, and chemistry. They were held first at the school level. The winners then progressed to the district level, then city, and then, in my case, to the Belarusian Republic level. Since my first Olympiads, I had been accustomed to winning. I had awards for all three subjects at most levels and didn't think much about it. In tenth grade, I got to the Republic Math Olympiad for the first time.

I clearly remember approaching the competition venue and listening to the conversations of the contestants. Most of them were boys, and many of them sounded extremely self-confident. The way they spoke, you'd think the diplomas were already in their pockets. At seventeen, I had one very bad trait—the fear of failure. I was so afraid of losing that I preferred not to try. Therefore, I left. I had not gotten too far when I bumped into my math teacher. Before I knew it, I was back to the venue, sitting alone at the desk.

At Olympiads of this level, the tasks were always very complicated, but this particular time, one task was especially difficult. When we came back the next day, we were told that only one person had gotten everything right. The names were hidden by assigned codes. Even when they read my code aloud, it took me a while to realize that they were talking about me. I was the only one to take first place that year.

I was never sent to the next level (the USSR Math Olympiad), though I was supposed to go there. One of the rumors had it that the son of a local organizer went instead of me. My parents were too timid to ask any questions about it.

My teachers at school made a big deal out of my victory. The main result of this episode was that I finally believed in my mathematical abilities and decided to become a scientist. In normal circumstances, I would most likely have achieved this goal.

Another exceptional teacher I had was a woman who taught me for ten years. She graduated from our

Vladimir Yul'evich Gurevich, Nella Abramovna Mazelson

university and came to teach at my school when I was in second grade. Since our school had no openings in the higher grades, she taught my class as an elementary school teacher for several years. Later, she was able to get a job according to her credentials, and she taught us both Russian language and Russian literature until we graduated. She was also the homeroom teacher in my class. She was as young and as enthusiastic as my math teacher, whom she married a year before our graduation.

We were "her kids," her first students, and she spent a lot of time with us. The standard literature textbooks at that time were written in a formal and much politicized language, which could kill the love for literature in anyone. The protagonists were either the typical representatives of the working class (which meant they were good) or the typical representatives of the bourgeois class (who were, of course, very bad). Usually, students did not have the freedom to express their own opinions. Everything was defined and decided for them. We had to write many compositions, and with many teachers, the topics— "Onegin as a typical representative of . . ." and "Class struggle in . . ." and so on—were extremely boring.

Our curriculum was cast in iron, but Nella Abramovna managed to inject some interest into it. She introduced us to books of memoirs written about great writers, and the authors became more human to us. We started seeing them as people with passions, mistakes, and beliefs. She encouraged me to write and often read my compositions aloud to the class. Most likely, when they later made their way to radio and TV, it was not without her help.

One of the brightest school memories for me is the performance she directed. We staged the scenes from Pushkin, and I played the role of Tatyana, the romantic heroine of *Eugene Onegin*. On the day of the performance, the costumes were brought for us from the TV station, and I was dressed in a nineteenth-century long dress. I also got a wig, which looked a lot like my own hair. I felt very romantic when I read the monologue of Tatyana, and the candle flickered on the table. Tatyana was writing a letter to a man she loved, expressing her feelings for him. For a woman to take the first step was unheard of in her time and not very common in my time either. I was certainly less brave than Tatyana was, and would never have done it, though I lived almost 150 years later.

The candle flickered, my voice trembled, and everyone applauded loudly. It was the highest point of my acting career, especially because it was the only one.

At that time, Soviet TV popularized the game of KVN, "Club of the Merry and Inventive." The teams (usually made up of students) competed by giving witty answers to questions, performing funny improvisations, and demonstrating their "homework"—funny sketches prepared in advance. These games became very popular everywhere and we had them too. I was the only girl on my school team and then on my city district team. I think I was invited for my erudition and ability to write. Our team was very successful, but then we lost the final game to another city district's team, and I remember crying about it.

The school years ended with a big bang: the graduation exams. We had exams in math (algebra, geometry, and trigonometry), physics, chemistry, Russian and English languages, Russian and Belarusian literature, history, geography, and social studies. My goal was to get a gold medal, which was supposed to help me enter the best university in Belarus. To achieve this goal, I had to get the highest marks in all subjects for every quarter of the last three years and get the highest marks on all exams. The exams were mostly oral. We had several days to prepare for each.

We studied together with my best friend, Valya. I remember days full of memorization of facts, dates, formulas, and equations. We studied at my place, and the days were full of food and chocolate, since my mom believed the latter boosted our memory. Whether true or not, the chocolate helped. Valya got her silver medal, and I got my gold.

Prom

I will end this part with a happy picture of my parents and me, taken before my prom. All the graduates (girls) had to wear white dresses. You guessed it right—my dress was made by my mom, only by that time she had a sewing machine.

The end of my school years in 1966 was also the end of my sheltered life. At seventeen, I entered the real world, and it was not always kind to me.

At seventeen, I entered
the real world,
*and it was not
always kind to me.*

PART 2

Between Two Lives

CHAPTER 25

Entering University

My husband teaches mathematics at an American research university. He is among the top researchers in his field. He is always supportive of his students, and after graduation, they usually find good positions in academia and industry. Even in his case, he often has difficulties attracting good PhD students, and almost all of them come from abroad. The profession of a math professor is one of the most prestigious in America, but Americans don't usually specialize in mathematics. People who have good analytical skills, which are essential for success in mathematics, often opt to become lawyers, doctors, or businesspeople. These occupations certainly pay much better wages.

This was not the case in the Soviet Union. For the Western reader, it is very hard to believe that medical doctors, dentists, and lawyers were among the lowest paid people there. In general, the disparity in salaries was minimal, which promoted a somewhat idealistic approach to the choice of a profession. Besides, PhDs were usually paid extra money for their degrees. There was always stiff competition to enter the mathematical faculty of a good university. This is understandable, and it may be a good thing. Unfortunately, the way the selection process went was neither good nor fair.

It was common knowledge that even for the brightest Jewish boys and girls, especially those not well-connected, it was almost impossible to get into the most coveted Moscow State University. Jewish students, and often even those who had only one Jewish parent, were asked significantly more difficult questions at the entrance exams than non-Jewish applicants. They were frequently assigned so-called "coffins" or "Jewish problems"—problems that most math professors would struggle to solve in a timely manner. A good illustration of such a "coffin" is that it took the legendary Andrei Sakharov, a brilliant nuclear physicist and a Nobel laureate, forty minutes to solve a problem that a Jewish boy had to solve during exam in ten minutes. Some of these problems had no solution at all.

There is a vast literature describing the discrimination of Jews at the Moscow State University. In the late seventies and early eighties, enthusiasts in Moscow created the alternative "Jewish People's University," an amazing institution where politics was strictly taboo and where Jewish boys and girls denied access to official institutions gathered to study mathematics.

When interrogated by the KGB, the creator of the Jewish People's University—Bella Subbotovskaya—explained its purpose with one sentence: "To give Jewish youth the opportunity to learn math."

In September of 1982, Bella Subbotovskaya died in a strange traffic accident, which many believed was a hit arranged by the KGB. The same year, two other human rights activists, Boris Kanevsky and Valery Senderov, who had self-published an essay called "Intellectual Genocide" devoted to this topic, were sentenced to years behind bars for this and other dissident activities. As one can see, mathematics was a dangerous business in the Soviet Union even in the beginning of the eighties, just before perestroika.

Of course, I had no idea at the time that mathematics and physics would be among the most "forbidden" professions for Jews, but many well-wishers told me that any attempt to enter the Moscow State University would be futile. I knew that the Belarusian State University in Minsk was also notorious for its discriminatory practices against Jews. Still, mathematics was what I liked best, and the word *Science* I always pronounced with a capital *S*, almost like the word *Poetry*. I naively believed that the combination of hard work and talent would overcome all obstacles. So I decided to apply to the Belarusian State University, the best higher education establishment in Belarus, conveniently located in my hometown. In the end, I was admitted into the Department of Mathematics at this university. My and my Jewish friends' entry exams did not differ from those given to the other students, but we did face attempts to give many of us lower grades than we deserved. In several cases, including those of my future husband Boris and myself, one man made a huge difference. Luckily for us, he was the head of the Examination Committee that particular year. The officials never made this mistake again. He was too decent and too honest to be trusted with such an important job. He intervened not only in my case, but also in many other cases and helped many of my fellow Jewish applicants. He was not afraid to take the side of a seventeen-year-old against some of his colleagues and to disobey direct orders from above.

When I became a student, this man would teach me calculus for two years. He was an extraordinary teacher whose lectures affected my whole perspective on mathematics. He was also an extremely knowledgeable and interesting man. Professor Yuriy

Professor Yuriy Stanislavovich Bogdanov
(photo from his department archives)

Stanislavovich Bogdanov deserves much more than a few words in my book.

Professor Bogdanov was born in 1920 into a family of Russian nobility, and his education and upbringing were shining through in his speech, in the way he carried himself, in everything he did. His collection of books included many first editions of Russian classics. A brilliant student of mathematics, he did not have time to finish his studies before the Second World War.

During the war, he served in the Red Army and, like many others, became a prisoner in a German concentration camp. He was wounded nine times, including a head wound. Later, during his imprisonment, he created an underground anti-Fascist group of fellow inmates. At the beginning of 1945, when his camp was liberated, he went to the headquarters of one of the United States ground armies, and they enlisted him. After the capture of the German town Jena, he was promoted to lieutenant in the United States Army and appointed commandant of Jena. Interestingly, because of his head wound, he couldn't wear a helmet and was allowed to wear a cap. Of all the high-ranking officials, only Dwight Eisenhower had the right to do this.

Bogdanov returned to Russia in 1945. On April 29, 1947, he was arrested on false charges of "criminal ties to American intelligence agencies." He was released from the Gulag in 1956, and only then was able to finish his studies.

One interesting detail: The man who interrogated Professor Bogdanov during his Gulag times was Jewish, a sadistic fiend who put out his burning cigarette butts on Bogdanov's forehead. For some people it would be a good excuse for anti-Semitism. Yuriy Stanislavovich was a bigger man than that, and he knew not to blame all Jews for this one man's crimes.

I realize that praising a man for not acting anti-Semitic may seem inconsequential to a person who grew up in a society free of any discrimination. Believe me, it was not trivial in the Soviet Union, where anti-Semitism was a governmental institution. Even less trivial was taking a stand and, in some sense, risking one's career by protecting Jewish boys and girls despite clear instructions from authorities.

As a gold medalist, I had to pass only two entry exams: oral and written mathematics. Professor Bogdanov intervened when my written exam got a lower grade despite being perfect. He also intervened when my future husband Boris faced an attempt by a notorious anti-Semite to lower his grade on the oral exam. As a result, we both got the highest grades and thus did not need to take any other exams. In September of 1966, I started my new life as a student in the mathematical department of the Belarusian State University.

CHAPTER 26

Agricultural Works

Recently, I stumbled upon an article in the *New York Times* that stated that in 1990 the authorities in the USSR abolished the old practice of compulsory potato harvesting by students and workers. It brought back many memories, which I decided to put on paper.

Since the beginning of Stalin's disastrous collectivization in 1928, which destroyed the individual farms and created large collective farms (*kolkhozy*), Soviet agriculture was becoming less and less productive. The most striking result of the collectivization was the Holodomor, famine in Soviet Ukraine from 1932 to 1933. Millions of Ukrainians perished in this disaster.

Official Soviet propaganda cited multiple reasons for the calamity, but never the main ones: the extermination of successful agricultural workers during the collectivization and the lack of interest and skills in collective farmers. Some historians believe that Stalin deliberately engineered the famine to eliminate the Ukrainian movement for independence.

The consequences of collectivization were felt even many years later, and not just in Ukraine. There was a well-known joke in my time: "This year our Soviet agriculture was again attacked by its four enemies: winter, spring, summer, and fall." To help fight the "enemies," or rather to gather the crops, the government sent people from cities and towns to collective farms. I don't think any economy can survive for long while sending professors, engineers, and physicians (even surgeons) to toil in the fields each fall, at the same time paying their salaries at their vacated respective workplaces. The cheapest available workforce of all were students.

I was not very good at agricultural activities, though I tried hard. Those of my university classmates who grew up in villages or in small towns where private houses had vegetable gardens were much more skillful than I was. In addition to my poor farming skills, I did not drink alcohol, valued my privacy, disliked vulgar jokes, and refused to pour out my soul to anyone who would listen. In other words, I was never a typical "builder of Communism" and, as a result, did not fit in well, was very aware of it, and felt extremely uncomfortable during these trips. On one of these trips, I got sick with severe food poisoning, and that was the end of my agricultural career. My husband (whom I will introduce in the next chapter), though, spent a month of each fall on a collective farm, all the while his PhD's salary was being paid to him by his research institute.

CHAPTER 27

Our Wedding

We are reaching the point in my book where "we" will often replace "I." I think it is time to introduce the man who became my husband and who will soon start appearing in every subsequent chapter.

When I first met Boris Mordukhovich, he was seventeen. Our university had special classes for schoolchildren interested in mathematics, and some of my school friends and I had been

My future husband

attending them since eighth grade. In November of our final school year, a new boy started showing up there. He was always dressed very formally, in a business suit and tie, looked somehow very anxious and very confident at the same time, and stuttered. Those who became acquainted with the very social and talkative

Boris later would never believe me, but this portrait is accurate. Another confession: For some reason, I really disliked him, called him a stuck up and a local genius, all behind his back. Girls at seventeen can be quite a pain, and I was not an exception.

One of my schoolmates was also attending these classes. Several months later, she decided to impersonate the Oracle of Delphi and prophesied that I would eventually marry Boris. I replied, "Him? Never!" Never say never; life loves to prove you wrong.

Eventually, we started talking a little. Boris played an important role in my university admission process. When my written examination paper got less than a perfect grade, Boris pushed me to go and challenge the verdict. I was very shy and would never have done it on my own. The paper was indeed perfect, and the grade was changed.

Boris also proved to be a fighter when he faced an attempt from a notorious anti-Semite to lower his grade on an oral exam and managed to fight it successfully.

My "Never!" didn't last very long. Persistence often pays off. Boris and I began dating when we were sophomores at the university. At the end of the third year, we got married. At that time, Boris was twenty-one, and I was twenty.

It was common to marry young in the Soviet Union. We may have been below average age, but not by much. By the time of graduation, and we studied for five years, many of our classmates were married, and some already had children.

There were some unique things about our wedding. Not every bride is warned by the groom's best man not to go ahead with the wedding. Boris and his best friend went on vacation together, and when they came back, this friend came to me and told me that Boris was impossible to live with. At that time, I naively believed that I could change anyone. We both were wrong. I didn't change Boris much but proved that anything is possible.

The shy bride

Our wedding pictures were unique too. I was a very shy bride, and this picture proves it. There exists another funny picture, with one of our classmates standing proudly between the newlyweds.

Another quite unusual feature for this time—we had a Jewish klezmer orchestra at the reception, and our multiethnic guests were all happily forming a ring and dancing one horah (a traditional dance performed at Jewish wedding receptions) after another.

In addition, if I had confessed that we spent our honeymoon in Crimea with three university friends, including the aforementioned best man, everyone would believe that this crazy couple had no future. Nevertheless, more than fifty years, two children, and six grandchildren later, we are still together.

Simultaneously with Boris, two more people entered my life and stayed there for a very long time. They are no longer with us, and the next two chapters are my tribute to their memory.

CHAPTER 28

Sholim Mordukhovich

My father-in-law

Sholim (Simche Sholom) was born and grew up in the city of Kremenchug in Ukraine.

Sarah Mordukhovich

His mother, Sarah Mordukhovich (née Braslavsky), died in 1940. My future father-in-law, her youngest son, was only sixteen at the time. His

Tevye Mordukhovich

family was so poor that young Sholim, who also went by Syoma, got a shirt made from his mother's shroud.

His father, Tevye Yaakov Mordukhovich, survived the war. He returned to Kremenchug and died there in 1962.

When the war started, Sholim was not even seventeen and had not finished high school yet. He volunteered, lied about his age, and because of his good grades, was sent to an artillery school.

He graduated from it in 1942 and, as a young lieutenant, spent the remaining years of war in the trenches. He belonged to the most vulnerable generation of those who fought. Here are the horrible demographic data: Of the men who were born in the Soviet Union 1923–1925 and who fought in the war, only three out of one hundred came back. Sholim Mordukhovich was born in 1924, and he survived. He fought heroically in many engagements, among them the bloody Battles of Kursk and Budapest. His final combat of the war was in the historic Battle of Berlin, in which he lost almost all of his friends—his regiment was practically wiped out there.

Senior lieutenant at twenty-one

He finished the war as a first lieutenant—highly decorated, brave, and handsome—and the only education he had was from that artillery school. His only choice was to become a career military man.

Sholim Mordukhovich was a capable and studious man. Pursuing a very challenging military career, traveling with his family from one small military settlement to another, he managed to graduate from high school, from the school of military translators, and then, finally, from the University of Foreign Languages—all by correspondence. He spoke very grammatically correct British English, using future past participle and future past perfect tenses much more often than is usual in present-day America.

It was very hard to pursue a military career for a Jewish officer, but he eventually reached the rank of lieutenant colonel. He would definitely have gone further if not for this major handicap—his ethnicity.

When he retired from the army and started his civilian career, I got to know him better. I realized that this always-silent man was well-read and very knowledgeable in many matters. He became a very kind and supportive father-in-law to me and a fantastic grandfather to our children. He loved spending time with them. Despite my objections, he always smuggled candy to them, allowed them to do whatever they pleased, and they adored him.

He was very hesitant to emigrate with us but very quickly got used to his new life. His mastery of the English language came in quite handy and he was always helping new Russian immigrants to fill out the numerous required forms and to adjust to life in the new country. Unfortunately, it did not last long. He died of cancer in 1993 at the age of sixty-eight, and his family and everyone who knew him grieved deeply. Our younger daughter still wears his wedding band close to her heart.

CHAPTER 29

Rosa Mordukhovich

When my dashing father-in-law came for a short visit to Moscow from Germany in 1947, he met a beautiful young woman, Rosa Lubarsky. Before meeting in person, they corresponded for at least a year, exchanging letters and photos. His visit to Moscow was a surprise to her. When he rang her doorbell, she was washing her hair, and came out wearing

Rosa Lubarsky

a robe and with a towel on her head. She immediately recognized him from the photos he sent her and slammed the door in his face. She took her time cleaning up, then opened the door again, and he was still standing there. They got married three days later, and had a chuppah arranged by her father, something for which her fiancé would have been kicked out of the army had the brass found out.

Men of Rosa's age and even years older were practically wiped out. Rosa lost every single one of her male classmates in the war. In her generation, most women either never got married or married men—often disabled veterans—ten to fifteen years older than themselves. When she had a graduation event from her university, her young husband happened to be in Moscow and came to it. She was the only one dancing with a man at that party; no one else had a male partner to dance with, and the young women danced with each other.

I believe there were two things that shaped Rosa's personality. The first one was the war— hunger, hardship, and the flight from a familiar home influenced all the children of war. Besides that, Rosa was the child of a very bitter divorce.

Alexander Lubarsky

Rosa's father, Zevel Nusievich Lubarsky, was a very talented man. He was very musical and charismatic, and women loved him.

He was a widower with four small children when he met and married Rochel-Leah Prikhozhaya. Rochel-Leah

Rochel-Leah Lubarsky

was from a well-off family whose fortune was taken away after the revolution. She and her two sisters worked as farm hands in someone's field, wearing potato sacks instead of dresses because they had nothing else. They managed to hide some of their mother's jewelry and sometimes exchanged them for food.

She had been married once before, but her first husband left for America promising to come get her and never returned.

After Rochel-Leah married Zevel Lubarsky, she became a mother to his four children. Her first child, a boy, arrived stillborn. The second one was their daughter Rosa.

Rochel-Leah was tiny, and she had a very difficult birth. When Rosa was born, she was so weak that doctors told Rochel-Leah that her baby won't survive. Some local women told her to put Rosa in a cow udder and if she turns blue, she'll die, but if she turns red, she'll survive. She and her sisters went to some farm, found some cow's udder, and put her in it. The baby immediately turned blue, and they all started wailing. Then they noticed she turned red, and ran back to the city with her. The udder was right: Rosa survived.

Rochel-Leah raised her daughter and her husband's children until the youngest of his children was sixteen. Then Zevel Lubarsky left Rosa's mom for a younger woman, and the children from his first marriage left home at the same time.

Rosa stayed with her less exciting mom. She saw her dad occasionally and always had to ask him for money to support them. There are divorces and divorces; this was a nasty one, and nobody spared the feelings of this little girl who loved her dad very much.

Zevel Lubarsky became Alexander Natanovich Lubarsky. He was a sharp dresser, never inquired about the price before buying something he liked, and could afford it while his former wife and his youngest child struggled to survive in poverty.

His brother organized and ran a business, which would be legitimate in any capitalist country, but, like any other private commercial activity, was outlawed in the Soviet Union. Alexander Lubarsky was caught selling refurbished watches. He was thrown into prison, where the interrogator and the guards, by his own definition, "played soccer with his head." When, severely beaten, he was thrown into the punishment cell, he saw the name of Rosa's mom on the wall. He decided that God was punishing him for what he had done to her. When released, he became very religious. He had a great voice, and eventually served as cantor in a synagogue in Lvov (now Lviv, Ukraine).

In 1962, he decided to immigrate to Israel and somehow got permission to do so. On the border, he and his wife were turned back with no explanation given. He returned to Lvov, suffered a stroke, and died.

Several years after his death, his third wife was allowed to immigrate to Israel. She later returned to the USSR to collect his remains and bring them to Israel. Zevel Lubarsky is buried in Jerusalem.

My father-in-law, who more than anyone else was affected by Rosa's explosive temper, always called his father-in-law "this jerk." Being extremely responsible and dedicated to his family, he could never forgive the man for abandoning his wife and ten-year-old child. My mother-in-law was an absolute monarch in her family, but when she saw her father or sent him money, it was done in total secrecy. Boris was thirteen when his grandfather died, but he never saw him, and Zevel Lubarsky never saw his grandson either.

For Rosa, it was a toxic mix: This childhood trauma, the war, hunger, and then evacuation from Moscow at sixteen.

She applied to the Moscow Pedagogical University when she turned seventeen and was accepted. She attempted to take a train to Moscow, and had some personal belongings and a large sack of flour with her. She was travelling next to a woman with a two-month-old baby who was trying to reunite with her husband. While changing trains, in the middle of nowhere, the woman handed the baby to Rosa and began moving her things onto the new train. All of a sudden, that train just started moving. A seventeen-year-old was left with a tiny baby in the middle of Bashkiria; her personal belongings were on the train with the woman. She ran to the head of the station, somehow the train was stopped, and they got Rosa and the baby on the new train. Once she got there, she realized that all of her belongings were stolen. The woman she was travelling with was too panicked about not knowing where her baby was to look after them. Since Rosa had nothing else with her, she returned to the "evacuation" village with the heavy sack of flour. She worked for a year, and then attempted to go to Moscow again. This time, she succeeded.

In Moscow, she stayed with relatives and had to sleep on the floor under the dinner table because there was no other place for her.

She became a student, but her only outfit consisted of a winter coat and soldier's boots. Because of it, she always sat in the last row and never spoke to anyone. After the first semester, they announced the names of the people who got perfect grades, and when they mentioned her name, everyone turned around to look for her because no one knew she even existed. She got a bigger stipend as a result of those perfect grades and used it to finally purchase a dress and some shoes.

When she married Sholim and had to follow her husband and move from Moscow to a tiny place in Belarus with horrible living conditions, she fell into a serious depression, which definitely influenced Boris's childhood and his personality.

Rosa Mordukhovich

The military was paid well in comparison with the rest of the population. Rosa never had to work outside of home. She was always very well-dressed, possibly compensating for her childhood and student years. She could afford nice vacations and custom-made clothes and had a husband who adored her, but it did not make her happy.

When I think about her formative years, it becomes easier to forgive her for being so difficult and to concentrate on her better and redeeming qualities, and there were many of those. She was very dedicated to her family. She was always very generous with both her money and her time. She helped me a lot when my kids were born and I had to go back to work, and she even helped her granddaughter Lena when her older great-grandchildren were born.

She was the proverbial Jewish mom to her only son Boris, but she nevertheless often made his life very difficult. One would think that she would be a stereotypical evil mother-in-law to me, but it was never the case. From the first time she saw me until her last moments, she was always my champion. If she overheard Boris raising his voice at me, she would scold him. She was constantly nagging me to spend money not on Boris but on myself, to buy expensive clothes and jewelry. My life near her was not an easy one, but she never attacked me personally.

When she became old, I became her advocate during her multiple stays in hospitals and rehabilitation centers. She was a fighter and beat the doctors' prognosis by many years. She lived to see her six great-grandchildren and made it to almost ninety-four, the oldest in our family. When she was dying, Boris was in Chile, and I stayed at her bedside for many days alone. Her last words, addressed directly to me, were "I always loved you. Honestly!" When Boris arrived, she was unconscious

Rosa at seventy

but immediately opened her eyes and called his name. We both spent her very last days with her, and I sincerely grieved for her. May she rest in peace; she did not have much of it here.

CHAPTER 30

Our Job Placement

Education in the Soviet Union was always free and very demanding. The system definitely did not spare any feelings of those who were less diligent or less obedient. We were deciding what we wanted to study when we entered university, and if we chose mathematics, as I did, we would study mostly mathematics. Our curriculum was predefined for us. There were no electives, and we could not refuse to study obligatory subjects like the History of the Communist Party of the Soviet Union or Scientific Atheism, whatever that means. It was extremely difficult to change our major or get a second education. You made your bed at eighteen, and you had to sleep in it for the rest of your life.

At the same time, professional education was often excellent, especially for good students. Of course, we had both outstanding and horrible professors, but to pass very rigorous examinations, you had to have some knowledge; in order to get the best grade, this knowledge needed to be substantial.

All students who passed the exams got stipends, but for those who got all the highest possible grades, these stipends were larger. As I described above, it was much harder for Jewish applicants to become students, but once we were in, most math professors graded us fairly. As a result, among those who graduated with honors, there was a significant number of Jewish students. The hardcover binding of a regular diploma was dark blue, but both Boris and I received the so-called "red diplomas" of high distinction. For any non-Jewish student, a red diploma meant a good career. For us, it was not the case.

In the Soviet Union, all college graduates went through obligatory job placements. After graduation, they were placed or "distributed" to a particular place of work, which could be anywhere in the huge country. The so-called "young specialists" had an obligation to work in this place for three years. During these years, they could not be fired and could not leave the job without a special permission.

We studied for five years, but our "distribution" happened at the end of our fourth year. To keep a semblance of propriety, the names of all three hundred students were arranged in a list, where our grades, extracurricular activities, and civic duties were all taken into account. This list was fair. Boris was number one, and I was number four. In theory, Boris could choose any of the available three hundred positions, and I could choose any but the three already chosen. In practice, it all happened very differently.

The situation with Boris was especially striking. Boris was not just a brilliant, straight-A student. He was also the chair of the university Student Scientific Society and came to his graduation with six published papers.

Professor Gabasov came to Minsk in 1967 from Sverdlovsk in the Ural region. He became chair of the newly founded Department of Applied Mathematics, and Boris became one of

Boris with Rafail Fedorovich Gabasov in Minsk (2016)

his students. Gabasov was thirty-two years old, young, energetic, and ethical. Boris worked very successfully under his guidance.

Rafail Fedorovich came to Minsk unprepared for the anti-Semitism at our university. Thinking of my life in the USSR, I often recall a quote from a famous poem by the Nobel laureate Joseph Brodsky: "If you happen to be native to an empire, better choose a distant province by the ocean." Sverdlovsk was not by the ocean, but even with all the state anti-Semitism, in the Urals, Siberia, Kamchatka, Azerbaijan, and some other distant places, Jews were often treated better.

Professor Gabasov was sure that with Boris's stellar record there would be no problem accepting him as a PhD student. Gabasov was a Tatar who knew a thing or two about the "fraternity of peoples" in the Soviet Union but did not realize the magnitude of the Jewish problem. He was shocked, tried to appeal to the provost and the president, and finally deemed further fighting hopeless. He tried to help Boris, but we were mostly on our own.

In our case, the situation was exacerbated by the existence of the residency permit (*propiska* in Russian). In short, everyone had a stamp in their internal passport certifying their permission to live in a certain place. *Propiska* was documented in local police registers, and people were prohibited from living or working anywhere without this permit. Acquiring it in big cities was very desirable and extremely difficult.

For an American reader, it is very hard to comprehend why big cities were so desirable. I love small, clean American towns where people know their neighbors and crime is rare. I currently live in a city of six thousand residents, which is a fifteen-minute drive from several major concert halls. This city has nice grocery stores, paved roads, and lots of wildlife as a bonus. In the Soviet Union, everything was measured by a distance from the nearest big city—Moscow, St. Petersburg, Kiev, Minsk, and other capitals of the Soviet republics. You could buy groceries in Minsk—yes, sometimes spending hours in lines, but still, you could. I cannot even find words to describe the life in many Belarusian or Russian small towns and villages: the roads, the houses, the drinking problems, the living conditions, the lack of indoor plumbing, and everything else. For people who were born and raised there, this life, I am sure, was familiar and possibly even somewhat attractive. Both Boris and I were typical city dwellers, born in the very downtowns of big cities. For us, it would be an exile.

The unmarried young specialists who were sent to the remote villages to teach retained their permit of residence and, after three years, could come back to live with their parents. We were married, and for us this exile would be lifelong.

As I mentioned earlier, we were both at the very top of the "distribution" list and in theory could choose any place we liked. In practice, it did not work this way. Before describing how it really worked, I would like to tell you one story that made this particular job placement especially difficult for Jewish students.

CHAPTER 31

A "Zionist Plot"

I was never a sports fan, so I do not remember whether this happened in 1969 or in 1970, who was playing against Israel in which basketball championship, and whether this game was shown on Soviet TV. The word *Israel* was always used in set phrases in combination with words like *aggressor* or *occupier*, and the word *Zionist* was considered particularly dirty. In my first years in the United States, I would never have believed that this word could become an obscenity on American campuses and among woke politicians. Nevertheless, it has happened and I am deeply saddened by it.

Going back to 1969, I remember very well a man who officially worked as a senior laboratory assistant in our department, but who in fact was the dean's assistant or secretary. He was a retired colonel of the Soviet Army and a well-decorated participant in the Second World War. He was also a rabid Communist and anti-Zionist. I still remember his open letters, which he published in the local newspaper. They always began with "I belong to a prominent Jewish family, but I angrily condemn . . ." Of course, he denounced the state of Israel, the

Zionist aggressors, the Israeli warmongers. It is interesting that in both countries, the Jewish anti-Zionists are always in bed with the anti-Semites, but it does not bother them at all. They never learn that when terrorists will come to kill the Jews, they will cut off their heads with the same barbaric pleasure they get cutting off the heads of their Zionist neighbors.

While writing this chapter, I researched this man and found an extremely impressive list of his military awards. He served in the artillery and was a real hero during the war. I remember his real name, but out of respect for his military service, I will call him by his initials—A. S. M. I will never understand what made him write those letters, as I will never understand American Jews who support BDS or Hamas. It is even harder for me to understand what made him do what I am about to describe.

Among our Jewish classmates, there was a young man who, I believe, was not very stable mentally. He was a good student but was capable of very weird, sometimes unreasonable, actions. After this basketball game, he approached A. S. M. and asked if the latter was rooting for Israel. The scared hero vehemently denied such a criminal thought, whereupon our classmate proudly declared that he did, in fact, root for the Israeli team.

This absurd story had huge consequences and negatively impacted many lives. Our heroic A. S. M. immediately informed either the local Communist Party bureau or the local KGB, and the witch hunt began. Our classmate was accused of Zionism, and the decision was made to expel him from the university. At a group meeting, two of his Jewish friends tried to defend him by explaining that he was not a Zionist, just a fool. From this moment on, the situation became a Zionist plot, a very serious offense. The two friends were marked for expulsion as well. I was always grateful that Boris and I studied in a different group; otherwise, it would probably have been our fate too.

To expel him, they needed a formal pretext and plotted to fail him in exams. One professor (V. F. Zhdanovich) refused to do it and was immediately fired. The Party secretary of our department was also fired for not being vigilant and missing a Zionist plot. The older brother of our hapless classmate was one of the few lucky Jews teaching at the university. You guessed it right; they fired him too.

The president of the Belarusian State University was a physicist and a notorious anti-Semite. He was not a war hero, so I do not see any need to protect his name. Anton Nikiforovich Sevchenko considered the Mathematics and Physics Departments his personal domains and actively took part in their "distribution." The year the "Zionist plot" happened, almost all Jewish students were sent to teach in the villages. We would be next and, as classmates of the "Zionists," we really had good reasons to worry.

CHAPTER 32

Our Job Placement (continued)

When the much-feared day arrived, we all gathered near the room where the printed list with the names of graduates was hanging on the doorpost, sorted in the order of their merits. I overheard one of our less pleasant classmates instructing another one: "Don't count the Jews who are ahead of you. What is your real number on the list?" He was definitely right; the Jews did not count. They were calling people into the room, everyone except Jews. More than two hundred people had already been "distributed." The best spots were taken. All the Jews were still waiting outside.

Later, we realized what was going on: Most likely, our dean, Aleksei Adamovich Gusak, was trying to avoid what happened a year ago. He was waiting for Sevchenko to leave the room. All of a sudden, it happened, and immediately they called us in, the first of all the Jews waiting outside.

When Boris and I entered the room, we saw representatives from various organizations fighting over the last non-Jewish student still in the room, a young woman with a pretty low GPA. That year, software developers were in high demand, and mathematicians with their good logical abilities usually made very good programmers.

What happened to me right after I entered the room did not seem funny then, but now I have to admit that it was quite comical. By that time, I still had not changed my last name officially at the university and was introduced by my maiden name, which was Jewish but not that stereotypical. My face is also far from being stereotypically Jewish, and I immediately became extremely popular with these recruiters. An HR representative from one of the academic research institutes was the fastest. He offered me a job at his institute, which I graciously accepted. We went together to the desk to fill in the documents, and there, to his horror, he saw that my father's name was Aron, which was indeed very Jewish. I have to give it to this man—he found a brilliant solution to his big problem. He feigned, albeit not very convincingly, a coughing fit and ran out of the room. This poor man never reappeared while I was there.

After that, everyone stayed still for a moment, and then a miracle happened. A man from the Heat and Mass Transfer Institute (HMTI) of the Academy of Sciences approached me and offered me a position. His name, as I found out later, was Roman Levitin, and he worked with the famous professor Teodor Lvovich Perelman. Perelman hired many Jews for his lab. I will write about his fate later.

Roman Levitin arrived at our "distribution" to fill in for a very important person from the institute. A woman who held a minor position in human resources accompanied him. She was in for a shock: For the nine positions he had to fill, Levitin hired not only me, but also three Jewish male students. All of them were at the very top of the list, all graduated with "red diplomas," all were our friends.

This woman was loudly lamenting her fate. "Everyone he signed up is Jewish! Prove to me that such and such [with a suspicious name] is not Jewish." I was consoling her, not at all surprised by her reaction, and too busy thinking about my incredibly good luck.

Since my scientific career ended very soon after that day, I will finish the story here, in this chapter. The whole next year, when we were supposed to write our senior theses, I spent at the Heat and Mass Transfer Institute. I was assigned to the lab of Professor Boris Berkovski and, working mostly independently, made some good progress. Professor Berkovski offered me the opportunity to become his PhD student, and I, of course, happily accepted his offer. My scientific future looked very rosy to me.

Four days before the official graduation date, the presidium of the Academy of Sciences wrote a formal letter to my university, in which they refused to accept several students who were placed with them. If you followed my story, you probably guessed it: The names of our three Jewish friends and my own name were the only ones mentioned in this letter.

I ran to the HMTI, hoping it was just a misunderstanding, but the people there had no idea that it even happened. They later told me that it was a direct order from the president of the Belarusian Academy of Sciences, N. A. Borisevich, a good friend of the aforementioned President Sevchenko of the Belarusian State University. It seems these two men were soulmates. Borisevich was also a physicist and a notorious anti-Semite. He did not bother for propriety's sake to add to the list at least one of our many non-Jewish classmates placed at numerous academic institutions. He knew that Sevchenko would fully appreciate and approve his actions. But, in fact, there were rumors that even Sevchenko himself was slightly taken aback by this.

Even now, fifty years later, I feel deep sadness writing about it. No one was fighting for me, though in all fairness, it probably would have been futile anyway.

Four days later, with the help of my dad, I found a grant-funded position at what is now called *Belarusian* State *Technological University (Technological Institute then)*. I ended up working there for seventeen very long years, right until our departure in 1988. Multiple times, I tried to change my job, and each time I was greeted by very welcoming HR people, but as soon as they had my passport in their hands, the position in question suddenly became unavailable.

I developed industrial control systems (ICS) for big enterprises, bringing serious money to my department. The money went to the heads of the department and multiple associate and assistant professors. Many of them never forgot to let me know that I was there because of their kindness. My boss wrote a PhD dissertation based entirely on my results. My award for my work was the trip to her PhD thesis defense in Leningrad and a stay at the beautiful historic Hotel Astoria.

My first project was developing an automated control system for a big potash plant in Soligorsk. Soligorsk was only seventy-five miles from Minsk, but it took me three hours to get there by bus. All of this was happening long before the era of personal computers in the USSR, and to debug the software, I had to take business trips to Soligorsk very often and debug it on their servers. I mostly got access to the computing machine late at night. My trip from the hotel to the computing center and back was usually quite a dangerous endeavor. Numerous drunken men had their own plans for how I should spend the night, and

I had several very narrow escapes. One night, a drunken guest of the same hotel tried to break open the door of my room, reassuring me all the time: "I won't touch you; I will just sit with you." The rooms did not have phones, and none of the multiple people who heard the loud banging interfered. The door survived, and I survived too.

Many locals worked in the mines. According to the census, in 1970, this very new city had thirty-eight thousand residents. I don't know what percentage of them were women. I only know that I seemed to be extremely popular there, and not in a good way.

When we finally got our own apartment, I always tried to come back home as early as humanly possible. I missed my family, always worried if I left them enough food, and an extra night in Soligorsk seemed like an unjust punishment. Boris could not leave little Lena home alone, and I had to walk from the tram stop to our apartment building. Once, I was coming home after midnight, and probably broke a world record in sprinting, running away from an obvious sex maniac who had been trying to grope me on the tram. I managed to exit the tram first and put some people between him and me. By the time he noticed me and ran after me, I was almost inside the apartment building, and luckily for me, the elevator was on the first floor. I was extremely scared, and ever since then, I have always been afraid to catch the last bus.

During my seventeen years at the *Technological Institute*, I moved from one project to another, from one department to another, but my job description stayed almost identical. My career peaked when I was twenty-five years old. I became a senior scientist, which was the highest position I could reach while my salary was paid by different grants. My bosses were always some associate professors who had no idea how the results were achieved. I stayed with this job until we emigrated.

All these years, I was also teaching students, earning some additional money, and getting a lot of pleasure in the process. Depending on the department where I was working at that particular time, I would teach a variety of subjects, most of which I had never studied myself. At the Department of Automatics, I taught computer programming and various computer languages, including FORTRAN. I taught economics when I worked at the Economics Department. I liked working with students, and they seemed to like me. I did not feel like a second-rate person when I was teaching, and students easily accepted my authority and, at the same time, spoke with me freely and even confided in me.

During perestroika, I finally managed to enter the graduate program for PhD studies. I did it while working full-time and raising two kids. I passed all my qualifying exams with the highest grades, and then we left the country. Funny enough, in my new country, even with my not-so-perfect English, my skills were in high demand, and I got offers after each of my job interviews. The country where I was born was not that kind to me.

Boris's thesis advisor Gabasov had connections at one research institution, which was working for the military. All he could do for Boris was to secure him a place there. Since nobody else wanted the class valedictorian, Boris became an employee of a semi-military institution. He had to be at work strictly on time, which in itself was a curse for my never-too-punctual husband. He had to program something in machine code. Trips to the bathroom were regulated. People were body-searched when entering and exiting the premises.

Fortunately for Boris, this place required a very high level of military clearance, and they were unwilling to bestow it upon a young Jewish man, despite his having a career-officer father and no relatives abroad. The same Professor Gabasov recommended Boris to a manager at the Research Institute of Land Reclamation and Water Management. Like mine, his career also peaked at age twenty-five, and our positions had identical names, except that, as a PhD, he got a higher salary. I will write more about his career in the USSR later.

What happened to me right after I entered the room did not seem funny then, but now I have to admit that it was quite comical.

CHAPTER 33

1971–1974

The year 1971 and the following years were hard not only for me. I would like to recreate the atmosphere of those years, when we started our post-university lives, by describing three unrelated events which happened in Minsk at that time.

At the beginning of the seventies, the pace of Jewish immigration to Israel started picking up, and several tragic events concerning Jews happened or almost happened at that time in Minsk. Some of these events were not a direct reaction by the authorities to the growth of Jewish self-awareness, but they were definitely a reaction by the anti-Semites to the increasingly hostile tone in the press toward the so-called Zionists. This term was again becoming a euphemism for the Jews. The coverage of the Israeli-Palestinian conflict was extremely biased (unfortunately, now much of the Western press is doing exactly the same). Immigrants to Israel were called traitors. The atmosphere was very charged.

Let me talk about the tragic events of the seventies in their chronological order.

At that time, there were still many famous, experienced, and even influential Jewish doctors in Minsk. Most of them belonged to the generation of our parents. The most famous endocrinologist at that time was Professor Naum Draznin, the father of Belarusian endocrinology. Neurosurgeon number one was Professor Efraim Zlotnik, the founder of the Belarusian school of neurosurgery and an uncle of our good friend. Both professors later immigrated to Israel.

The most celebrated urologist was the creator of the Belarusian urological school, top operating urological surgeon, and brilliant researcher named Abram Iosifovich Mikhelson. On March 19, 1971, the sixty-nine-year-old Professor Mikhelson was shot at point-blank range. A man in a raincoat was waiting for him on the stairs of the urological department at the Minsk Regional Hospital. Professor Mikhelson asked the man if he wanted to see him and, after the affirmative reply, told him to come back on Wednesday. The man took out a hunting rifle from under his raincoat and opened fire. The murderer aimed not to wound but to kill: He used the ammunition for bear hunting. Professor Mikhelson got multiple wounds, thirteen of them to his stomach. He managed to get to his office with the words "He killed me."

The time was 3:00 p.m., and the office was full of his colleagues and his former and current students. The surgery started right away. There were two teams operating on him simultaneously. The surgeons were operating on his stomach, and an orthopedic surgeon—his friend Professor Marks—was trying to repair his shattered elbow. His case was hopeless from the very beginning. They knew it but had to try.

The murderer was arrested the same evening while he was watching TV at his nephew's apartment. His rifle was hidden under the bed. "I did what I wanted," the man said calmly. Professor Mikhelson had seen this man a year prior at his clinic. The killer forgot his face but remembered that the doctor was a Jew. The killer had an adenoma of the prostate (BPH), but believed that he had cancer. He wrote multiple letters to the Ministry of Health, complaining that Jewish doctors were trying to kill him and threatening to take action against them.

The psychiatric evaluation after his arrest proved him fit to stand trial. At court hearings, the killer used the phraseology of 1952; he spoke of the "killers in white coats." Soviet doctors always wore white coats, and this phrase was coined and widely used during the infamous Doctors' Plot in the fifties. In such a way, two decades later, that Stalinist campaign backfired in Minsk.

Professor Mikhelson had saved so many people that his funeral was attended by a massive crowd. His colleagues, his numerous former patients, people he helped—all of them came to say goodbye to a great doctor. An influential and grateful former patient even sent a military orchestra. The family was allowed to choose the cemetery. His monument was created by the famous architect Leonid Levin, whose name I will mention again in this book.

I read in the memoirs of Professor Mikhelson's daughter that, after his death, the monograph he spent a lot of time coauthoring was published without his name. Only one Belarusian newspaper hinted that his death was a tragedy; all other printed obituaries spoke about his "premature death."

The next tragic event happened several months later, in March of 1972. There was a huge explosion at the Minsk Radio Factory. The true number of casualties was kept secret, but the whole building collapsed, and there were definitely more than one hundred people killed and 250 injured. The real cause of this tragedy was a poor ventilation system and the spontaneous combustion of the dust.

The relatives of those killed were not getting any answers from the authorities, and almost immediately, a rumor arose that there was not a single Jew among the dead which, of course, meant that the Jews must have caused the explosion. The same rumor was being spread after September 11 in America. Another rumor, reminiscent of the Doctors' Plot, was that all the Jewish doctors didn't come to work on the day of the explosion.

At night, a crowd of several hundred people, thirsting for blood, headed for Shevchenko Boulevard, where many Jews from the recently demolished houses of the "Jewish" Nemiga Street, in the former ghetto area, had received their new apartments. This time, even the KGB was scared of the imminent pogrom and brought additional police and KGB troops to the city. Although the police promptly dispersed the rioters, I read that for a long time some Jews in Minsk kept axes by their apartment doors, scared of the sudden animosity of their neighbors.

Strangely enough, I learned about this potential pogrom only years later. Recently, I read that some Jews at that time joined hunting societies in order to acquire guns. I am sure those who knew about it began thinking about emigration long before we did.

In the previous chapter, I promised to write about the tragic fate of Professor Perelman, whose PhD student I was once supposed to become. In December of 1974, Jewish Minsk was rocked by yet another horrible newsflash: The physicist who headed the laboratory of the Heat and Mass Transfer Institute, Professor Teodor Perelman, was killed in his own apartment. Many Jews, passing by building number 76 on Leninsky Prospekt, where Synthetics clothing store was located in those days, slowed down their steps and peered with fear into the obvious traces of fire on the eighth floor.

There are almost no publications about this event, and many details are still unknown. The consensus is that the murderers poured something highly flammable at his door and set it on fire. When the flaming liquid, gushing under the burning door, set fire to the hardwood floors, Perelman tried to help his son get over to the adjacent balcony. He managed to save the son, but was himself overwhelmed by the toxic fumes, fell from the eighth floor to the ground, and died.

The official investigation found neither the arsonist nor the cause of the fire. Unofficially, people were whispering that napalm was used and that it was a professional hit. Those close to Professor Perelman knew that he had received many threats before. There was gossip that this was due to the departure of some of his Jewish staff to the United States and Israel. The KGB was spreading rumors that he was killed by the Zionists because he refused to immigrate to Israel. I never saw anything published in the newspapers then. I still see almost nothing on both the Russian and Belarussian Internet, besides some references to his articles, and I was unable to find any photos of him.

A brilliant physicist, at the time of his death Professor Perelman was only forty-one.

The death of Perelman affected all of us. He lived in the very downtown of Minsk, in the area where many people shopped, went to see movies, or just passed through on public transportation. I remembered him from my year at the Heat and Mass Transfer Institute, and even many years later, I would lift my eyes and search for the long gone traces of fire on the façade of his house. I remembered and searched but still went with the flow of my everyday life, dreaming about finding a better job and mostly about my own apartment.

CHAPTER 34

A Home Of Our Own

In the Soviet Union, there were several ways for a young couple to live separately from their parents. We could "build" a cooperative apartment, but such an opportunity was not easy to find; besides, it was very expensive, and we definitely could not afford it. We could rent a room at someone else's apartment, but demand exceeded supply, and to exchange living with your own parents for living with strangers did not seem like a good idea. The most practical way was to join a long waiting list for a government apartment, distributed, if you were lucky, through your workplace.

To be eligible for improvement of the current living situation, people had to have in their current dwelling a certain very small amount of living space per person. We easily met this requirement. Fortunately for us, Boris's workplace had such a list (mine did not), and our wait had begun. By the time Boris reached the top of the list, we had already been married for eight years.

There were certain rules that were usually observed. A family of two would get one room. A family with one child (like ours at that time) would normally get a one-bedroom apartment. People with PhDs or other advanced degrees were eligible for an extra room. The apartment that became available was small by Western standards, but almost luxurious by ours. Its size was 39 square meters, or 420 square feet, and it had two bedrooms. For us it was a dream apartment, a way to live independently as a family.

Perhaps it would have gone more or less smoothly, but the next person on the list was a brother of one of the very big shots in the Communist Party structure. The law was on our side, but no one cared about the law in this lawless society. The next apartment could arrive in another two or three years and be a one-bedroom in a much worse location.

Everyone but Boris considered the situation hopeless. He again proved to be a fighter and began looking for a way to defeat the corrupt system.

One of his old friends was a prosecuting attorney, a good man who was on our side. He saw a clear violation of the law, really wanted to help, but said that the only people who could potentially override the local Party Committee were the superior Party functionaries. "Try to find a personal connection with someone," he said. "Otherwise, it's all hopeless."

Before proceeding, I have to explain to my Western readers the abbreviation Komsomol. Komsomol was a Soviet organization for young people aged fourteen to twenty-eight. It was primarily a political organ for spreading Communist ideology. After its founding in 1918, young people joined it willingly. In my time, many young people joined the Komsomol because those who stayed away usually were denied spots at good schools and universities.

No one in our family had any connection with the Party functionaries. I was preparing myself for several more years of living with my parents. Then Boris had a bright idea. He remembered that when he was a teenager, he knew one young woman who curated their high school and was the secretary of the Komsomol District Committee. At that time, they both lived in a small military-base town. A direct career path for a Komsomol functionary was to become a Communist Party functionary. What if this woman had built a successful career? What if she was in Minsk and remembered him?

Because she had since married and changed her last name, it was not easy to find her, but Boris managed it, and she recognized him. This woman's authority trumped the authority of our competitor's brother. To make a long story short, her interference eventually helped. Also, it was very difficult to buy French perfume, but I had one unopened bottle and treasured it. This bottle made an excellent "thank you" gift, everyone was happy, and we moved into a new apartment.

We had a living room, a bedroom/study (which was mostly a library with bookshelves), a desk for Boris, a folding sofa bed for us, and also a small room for our Lena. The kitchen was only 64 square feet, but I finally had my own kitchen, and Lena—who was five at the time—was not sleeping in the same room with us anymore. As was usually the case, this apartment had only one bathroom.

Furnishing the apartment was also an adventure. Through some connections, we were able to buy furniture and a piano for Lena. Boris bought a color TV set in Moscow and managed to bring it home, first on a train, and then in a big truck he flagged at the railway station. I was afraid that he would become too pushy, but this storm of activity stopped with the TV.

Everything else was a hunt, and besides hunting for groceries, I was hunting for dishes, for nicer linens, for all kind of things, feeling very happy to finally be my own person, the lady of the house. We spent eight years in this apartment, all the time waiting in line for a phone to be installed. We moved out still "unconnected," and all these years we relied on the kindness of our good-hearted neighbors, who did have a phone line, when it came to emergencies.

By the time Boris reached the top of the list, *we had already been married for eight years.*

CHAPTER 35

Everyday Life

When we moved into
our own apartment, my life
became happier in some
respects and more difficult
in others. It was the life of a
typical Soviet woman who
worked hard and had kids.

Every working day usually
began very early for me. I
had to cook breakfast for my
family, eat mine as quickly
as humanly possible, and
prepare Lena for her day, first
in kindergarten and later at

Lena in kindergarten (1978)

school. At that time, I was a night owl and hated the sound of
our alarm clock. My favorite meal is still a quiet breakfast when
I do not have to rush anywhere.

Storming the tram in the morning rush hours required many
skills, which I soon acquired. I had to calculate as precisely as

possible where the tram doors would stop. Then I had at least some chance to get inside. All the men's chivalry was gone, and I was always entering the tram with several men pushing me or holding onto my back. This routine offered many opportunities for sexual predators, and I once almost broke the finger of one of them.

The lunch break I always spent very productively. After quickly eating whatever each of us brought from home, the women (and sometimes men) went hunting for food. If we saw a line forming near a store, we would jump to the end of the line before inquiring what people were queuing for. On a lucky day, I could buy meat, or chicken, or sausage, or fruit, or imported canned vegetables, or—on very rare occasions—fresh fish. We always canned fresh fruits and berries and prepared jam in the summer to provide some vitamins in the winter, since fresh fruit was available only in season.

Let me talk for a minute here about a Russian-style string bag. The Russian word for it was *avos'ka*, which can be translated as "maybe-bag." The word was introduced in 1935 by the famous Russian comedian Arkady Raikin: "Here is my maybe-bag. Maybe I'll get something into it . . ." Even the most stylish women usually had a string bag in their purses. Quoting George Orwell, the exceptions were only those who were "more equal than others."

If I bought something exciting, a part of it usually was stored or frozen for the next big celebration, either a birthday, or New Year, or something equally important. Russian hospitality was proverbial, and it was amazing how much food was on the table for the guests. Soviet women achieved this abundance by freezing fresh food and storing up on canned food for months in advance.

Hunting for food was almost an everyday chore, but besides eating, people needed to dress, furnish their apartments, buy books, and fulfill many other needs. It was an even more complicated task, unless you wanted to settle for the ugly stuff available in our stores every day.

Until recently, my fellow Americans were unfamiliar with any shortages. If there was demand, there was supply, as simple as that. When the pandemic started, there was a shortage of toilet paper and paper towels. Do those who were born here remember their joy when they managed to buy or order the much-needed toilet paper? In the Soviet Union, we often experienced this sort of happiness. We were happy when we bought fresh fish (not the frozen tasteless variety), young chicken, or edible sausage. However, when we bought imported shoes, or dresses, or even Soviet children's tights, we were beyond happy; we were exhilarated.

By the way, toilet paper was always scarce, so people bought as much as they could at once. You could often see an elegant woman or a serious man out in the street wearing a toilet paper necklace for everyone to envy.

It will be hard to explain this to a Western woman, but I once bought Finnish winter boots two sizes bigger than I needed. When it was my turn to buy, my size was gone. After two hours spent in line in the cold, among angry women, I could not just leave. Besides, I really needed warm winter boots. I wore these big boots for years with two pairs of warm hand-knitted wool socks. If I remember correctly, they even immigrated with me to the United States, and I wore them our first winter there. The next year I could afford to buy new well-fitting boots.

When you cannot buy it, you make it. I taught myself to sew and to knit, and all of us were wearing my creations. I sewed a jacket for Lena that was so chic it looked like it came from abroad. We were both very proud of it.

Out of necessity, I learned to knit even the most complicated patterns almost without looking and was able to knit and read at the same time. I once tried to do it on a train, but it attracted so much attention that I never did it again in public. Knitting at home was different. Being an avid reader, I never had time to do just that. Reading and knitting was not a waste of time; my conscience was clear, and I knitted a lot. The white dress I wore in the photo in chapter 10 was knitted by me, and so were many others. Despite all the shortages, and because of my efforts, we were all dressed presentably. Unfortunately, I never learned to make shoes.

After work, I stormed the tram again, trying to bring Lena home from preschool as soon as possible. Being there was not a very happy experience for my child. In general, getting a place in a preschool close to home was a huge success. We managed to do it by offering a good "gift" to one of our well-connected neighbors.

Luckily, our Lena encountered anti-Semitism only later, when she went to school. She had the regular day care experience of a child whose parents didn't have any connections and were "useless," unlike some people in retail or medical professions. There was one preschool teacher and one assistant for more than forty active children, whom they had to feed, dress for every outside activity, and even teach something. Lena was a very obedient child, and her main sin was her inability to sleep during the mandatory after-lunch nap. Nevertheless, she was not very happy there, and I will never forget

Mom-daughter time

the sight I saw every evening when I ran from the tram stop to the preschool: My shy daughter jumping up and down in the window, screaming for the whole world to hear: "Mommy, mommy! My mom is here!"

What a joy it was to hug her and to play with her on the way home, pushing each other into tall snow piles, making up stories, laughing, and enjoying each other's company. At home, we would always prepare our dinner together, and she willingly assisted me in almost every chore I had to do.

I will never forget our long walks through the city parks and the forest together. Lena still remembers the stories I invented for her when we were together.

Father-daughter time

Boris was spending all his free time on mathematics. His solo walks with Lena were rare, but she still vividly recalls each one of them and each story he told her.

Remaining an authority figure for Lena, I by some miracle managed to become her friend, or rather she managed to become a good friend to me. I believe that this relationship stays the same even today.

Very early in life she became as protective of me as I was protective of her. My favorite recollection is how, when she was five, she told me, "Mom, I really worry when you cross the road without me." When bad things were happening to me later in life, Lena was always by my side, working hard together with my tired but very experienced guardian angel to save me.

Lena's early childhood was very sheltered and very happy. Besides loving parents, she was blessed by two sets of doting grandparents who were always involved in her upbringing. She was very trusting, finding good in everything and everyone, always ready to help and share her toys and her food.

Spoiled by my own school experience, I never suspected that her first school year would be very different. Her first-year teacher was highly decorated, and it took me a while to realize that something was very wrong. Children often don't tell their parents when someone, especially a teacher, is bullying them. If something does not go well, children blame themselves. I learned many years later that this teacher was repeatedly mocking Lena and putting her down in front of the class. She always denied Lena's request to go to the bathroom while other children were allowed to go. Lena was bringing home less than perfect grades, and I thought that her teacher was extremely strict with everyone. Even now, I blame myself for not reading the signs earlier. By the end of her first grade, the once happy, bubbly child had dark circles under her eyes and began to stutter. She also received the lowest grade possible for behavior, something that was very hard to explain given Lena's obedient and quiet nature. Only then did I realize that we were dealing with a person who hated my child and was trying hard to destroy her.

As I wrote earlier, I am not a confrontational person, and I am not always proud of it. I sometimes let things slide, even when it would be better to make my position very clear. I believe my first real confrontation ever was with this teacher. Since in the Soviet Union the same teacher usually taught the first three or four grades of elementary school, I had no choice but to transfer Lena to another school. If the first one was located very close to where we lived, to get to the second one, an eight-year-old had to cross a very busy road. Our working days started much earlier than her school, and I remember teaching her to attach herself to some older woman and, of course, to always obey the traffic lights. Since the drivers often disregarded all traffic signals, I was forever afraid that something would happen and relaxed only when I got home after work. It was very typical at that time for the children to walk to school alone, come back to an empty apartment, and open it with their own keys, worn like pendants hanging around their necks. Out of necessity, our children became independent at a very early age.

Besides being a rabid anti-Semite and a sadist, Lena's first grade teacher was not just a Communist; she was a zealot. Lena regularly came home from school with many stories right out of *Pravda*, the infamous official newspaper of the Communist Party of the USSR. Boris and I had a conversation and decided that, though it could be dangerous for us, we didn't want to let this propaganda influence our child. We asked Lena not to repeat what we were saying, but since that day, most of our replies to Lena's reciting at home of her teacher's opinions started with the word *actually*. We trusted our child, and she never made us regret it. Since then and until this day, politically, we have usually been on the same page.

We were luckier with Lena's second-grade teacher. She cared about our daughter, and a couple of weeks into the new school year she summoned me to school to ask if we beat Lena at home for poor grades, having no other explanation for why Lena was panically afraid whenever she so much as looked in her direction. Lena's stutter disappeared very soon, and I saw my smiling, happy child again. Only many years later, I found out that, in the new school, Lena was involved in many altercations, sometimes physical, and the reason was always anti-Semitism.

All these bad experiences did not break her but made her stronger. Lena is still kind and generous to a fault. At the same time, she is a fighter, and I could not be more proud of her.

CHAPTER 36

Zhdanovichi

For big city dwellers, it was customary to bring their children to the countryside every summer. Since Lena was one and until our emigration, we brought first Lena and then both our kids to the village to avoid hot summers in the dusty and polluted city.

The small village called Zhdanovichi, fifteen minutes by train from central Minsk, was an ideal place for renting a room or two in a rustic wooden dwelling and still being able to go to work in the city every day. We could buy fresh milk there; fresh air was free; and a dry pine forest was a good place for gathering wild strawberries and blueberries, mushroom picking, and hanging our hammocks. On June 1, we usually rented a truck, loaded it with some furniture, pillows and blankets, pots, pans, and dishes and left the urban civilization for three months.

The houses in the village did not have indoor plumbing. There was a well with a bucket on a chain in every yard. One could crank the handle and get water by hand. A primitive outhouse shyly stood in the far corner of the yard. The chickens were taking their dust baths in the sun. A handsome rooster was singing very early in the morning, cheerfully announcing one more beautiful

The house where we spent fifteen summers with our children

day. He had a very annoying habit of not finishing his crowing, stopping at "COCK-A-DOODLE . . ." The feeling that something was wrong and the expectation that he would soon finish it woke us up more than the crow itself.

During the summer months, the owners lived in a small cottage in the yard. A big furry sycophant dog named Friendie (Druzhok) was chained to a doghouse. He knew really well how to earn his keep and barked like crazy, but only if someone visited us when the owners were home. As soon as the owners left, he could not care less. Despite his name, he was not very friendly. Still, we saved all the meat bones for him. Once, there was a very strong wind, and my drying laundry flew all over the yard. Friendie looked very cute in my pink lacy nightgown.

It often rained, and then the streets were full of mud. Our rubber boots and raincoats were a crucial part of our rather minimalistic wardrobes. We had to bring groceries from the city. The village had its own small food store, but like nearly all village stores, it sold mostly canned food, beer, cheap fruit wine, and vodka. Since most of us didn't own cars, we first carried the bags with the groceries to the train station in Minsk, and then from the railway station in Zhdanovichi to the village houses where we rented rooms. Still, primitive living conditions did not worry those of us who did not own dachas but still wanted to spare their children from spending whole summers in the big city.

This is probably a good time to mention the important role of the institution of grandmothers in the Soviet Union. Most women in my generation had professional careers. For one thing, it was very difficult to survive on only one salary, but there was also another reason—society frowned upon stay-at-home moms. Women made up a sizable proportion of engineers, doctors, economists, and health care workers. They were teachers or worked in retail, in cafés and restaurants, in construction. At the same time, childcare was not easily available and often substandard; nannies were very hard to find and most young families could not afford to pay them anyway. A grandmother (*babushka* in Russian) was often the center of the family, the person who took the primary responsibility for the children's upbringing.

There was a clearing in the woods, which was a gathering place for all families spending their summers in this village. Many years later, we visited Zhdanovichi, and in the middle of the summer, this clearing was empty. In our time, it was full of life. I don't know why it happened this way, but many families coming there for the summer were Jewish. My only plausible explanation is that non-Jewish families often had relatives in the villages farther afield, and they could send their kids for the summer there. The locals tenderly called this place "the Yids' woods." During the day, one could see many grandmothers watching their precious grandchildren there. In the evenings and during the weekends, grandmothers went home to rest, by which time the younger people, the parents now in full charge of their children, would occupy the clearing.

In Zhdanovichi, we've found much more than just fresh air. There, we've found friends for life.

The Little Red Riding Hood

We were young and not always serious. We wrote songs, poems, sonnets, plays, and even a short opera and performed them in the same forest clearing. The picture above shows a scene from a slightly adapted version of *Little Red Riding Hood*.

Our children

We organized carnivals for our children, and they remember them to this day. We had soccer games and bonfires. When our children were asleep, we sometimes left them with their sleeping grandmothers and sneaked into the same forest to sing, dance, drink Bulgarian dry wine, and talk. Not that we preferred Bulgarian wine to, let's say, French, but it was the only dry wine available.

Basilio the Cat and Alice the Fox

In this picture, our daughter Lena is Basilio the Cat and her friend Alla Averbukh is Alice the Fox from the Russian children's book *The Golden Key, or The Adventures of Buratino*, based on the famous Italian novel *The Adventures of Pinocchio* by Carlo Collodi. Thirty-three years after our departure, Lena and Alla are still best friends.

Our political views also united us. We all despised the totalitarian political system we had to live with. In a country where KGB informants had infiltrated most circles of friends, it usually took some time to get to know people before you started discussing politics with them. We did not suspect each other; we simply presumed that everyone who hung the hammock in our clearing was a friend and a like-minded person.

We are still friends, or more than that, we are family, and our family is growing now on American soil. In this picture, which is sadly missing our Irina, the founding fathers and mothers are wearing green T-shirts that read "Seasoned in Zhdanovichi."

Our growing family

Blue T-shirts proclaim "Made in Zhdanovichi" and are worn by our children who grew up there. And the orange ones say "Zhdanovichi what?" and adorn the spouses and children of the Zhdanovichi kids.

We still write songs and poems and have carnivals, and the best part of me writing skits again is the stars performing in them—my own granddaughters.

CHAPTER 37

Simchat Torah

My husband and I recently went to a synagogue in Ann Arbor for a Simchat Torah celebration. When I watched my gray-haired husband dance with the Torah, tears started streaming down my face. I suddenly vividly remembered how we, still very young, went every year to a small wooden building that was the only synagogue in Minsk and danced there in the yard, knowing very well that our pictures were taken by KGB men. What was I crying for? For the years that passed, for our youth spent in a totalitarian country, for many other things but certainly not because I missed the KGB agents.

At that time, Jewish life in Minsk for people like me was almost nonexistent. There were Jewish activists in Minsk who were fighting for permission to immigrate to Israel. They tried to revive Jewish culture and distributed samizdat (I explained this word earlier, in chapter 23). Though I personally knew one of the members of this group, I did not know any details about their activities, considered myself a person of Russian culture, and emigration was very far from my thoughts. I very much regret it now; it would probably have given my life a different purpose. There are several points in a long road called life where the road branches out, and like in Russian fairy tales, "you go left—your horse is killed; you go right—you meet a beautiful princess, or rather prince in my case; you go straight—you meet your death." I sometimes ponder what would happen if I took a different route, though I realize how completely pointless it is to wonder.

In the seventies, Simchat Torah celebrations were almost the only times when I saw a group of Jewish men and women as a unit, as a part of the nation of Jewish people—the Jews. On regular prayer days, the synagogue was almost empty; it barely had a minyan, a quorum of ten men required for Torah reading and certain other religious obligations. Even on High Holidays, the absolute majority of those attending were old men, who probably studied Torah in their youth, just as my dad did. On Simchat Torah, though, it was a magnet, a gathering place for at least some young people who expressed their Jewish identity by coming there despite all possible repercussions, danced the horah, sang, and felt happy and somewhat courageous.

CHAPTER 38

The Pit (Yama)

In the Minsk of my time, there was a very modest Holocaust memorial erected inside the Pit where the Nazis murdered five thousand Jews from the Minsk ghetto. Five thousand were executed in this particular place. Altogether, the population of the Jewish ghetto was between eighty thousand and one hundred thousand, and almost all of them were killed. The monument was erected with private donations from Jewish citizens, my hungry parents among them. It had an inscription engraved on it, which was written by the Yiddish poet Chaim Maltinsky.

Chaim Maltinsky lost his family in the Minsk ghetto. He valiantly fought in the war and lost a leg in the battle for Berlin. Even so, getting permission to place a very innocent engraving in Yiddish on a monument was not simple. Maltinsky had to climb on his one leg to the sixth floor of the Government House to visit the office of the Main Directorate for the Protection of State Secrets in the Press under the Council of Ministers of the USSR, abbreviated as Glavlit— the main censorship agency in the USSR. He begged the censor to permit the Yiddish inscription on the monument to murdered Jews: "A bright memory for eternity to five thousand Jews who died at the hands of the fiercest enemies of humankind—Nazi-German villains on March 2, 1942."

In the eyes of the censor, there were two problems with it: The inscription was written in Yiddish and the word *Jew* was explicitly mentioned. The censor, who also fought in the war, first denied the request, but even censors sometimes have hearts. He relented after Maltinsky said that he just wanted to honor the memory of his mother, wife, and seven-year-old son killed in the Minsk ghetto. The monument was built and unveiled in 1947, the first and for many years the only one with a Yiddish inscription in the Soviet Union. It was cut from an old tombstone by the Jewish stonecutter, Mordukh Sprishen.

In 1949, Chaim Maltinsky and Mordukh Sprishen were both arrested and sent to the Gulag: Maltinsky "for trying to sell the Far East and part of Siberia to the Americans" and Sprishen for his collection of Jewish recordings, all of them officially published in the Soviet Union. KGB goons certainly let their imagination run wild. Maltinsky was a Yiddish poet and the only thing he could sell was his wooden leg.

At the end of the sixties, a group of Jewish activists came to the Pit to clear away the garbage around it. In the early seventies, a group of dissidents organized a meeting there on Victory Day. It quickly became a tradition, and hundreds of Jews came to this monument every May 9 instead of going to the official Victory monument in the center of the city on Victory Square. We, like many others, have also adapted to this tradition. Every year, I was very excited to be there, honoring the memory of people who perished in the ghetto, being part of an ancient people and proud of my heritage.

Veteran of the just war

There was something unbelievably touching about seeing the Second World War veterans, my dad among them, with all their decorations pinned to their jackets; grandmothers holding the hands of their grandchildren; young men and women in their holiday best. This was the place to show that we still exist, that we have our dignity, and that we can even be a force when we are united.

The Soviet officials fought back. They built a huge apartment complex next to the Pit, taking up a lot of space from where the crowd could gather. They brought powerful loudspeakers which played peppy military marches so loudly that people could hardly talk with each other, let alone make public speeches.

I recently found out that there was a plan to fill up the Pit and build a trivial park with benches on top of it, thus burying both the mass grave and the monument. The Pit and the black monument were saved by one man, David Kanonik, a former prisoner of the Minsk ghetto who lost thirty-two of his family members in the Pit. This man not only collected more than eight hundred signatures against this "project," he managed to pass the information and the notebook with the signatures to Israel. When the Israeli radio station Kol Israel reported that Minsk wanted to demolish the first monument to the murdered prisoners of a ghetto in the USSR, the information was immediately picked up by the BBC, Voice of America, and other foreign radio stations. It started a real commotion in Minsk—the authorities didn't know what to do. Finally, after several days of silence, the Party Central Committee issued a command to retreat.

I vividly remember how one Victory Day we stood in a long line of people who wanted to lay flowers on the mass grave. Our little daughter Lena was holding flowers in her hands. When we approached the monument, I realized that there was a man behind it with a big photo camera who took pictures of everyone approaching. Look at him; he is hiding behind the monument in this photo. I smiled and let him take my picture. I am not the bravest person in the world, and I knew perfectly well that this man worked for KGB. Still, it was an exhilarating moment when I felt that in my own little way I was doing the right thing and teaching my child a very valuable lesson. I am sure that hundreds of people had shared this feeling with me.

People laying flowers at the monument
(photo by Hanoh Feldman)

We were just a typical Jewish family who lived in Soviet times. I am not ashamed of our past, but we were not heroes. Heroes were those outstanding people who actively fought for national dignity and for the right to emigrate. It is hard to believe that they had to fight even for the right to gather at mass graves where massacred members of their families were buried.

Among them were three retired colonels of the Soviet Army, three heroes of war—Lev Ovsishcher, Efim Davidovich, and Naum Al'shansky (my dad's landsman, whom I saw at least once at my parents' dinner table). Davidovich died from a heart attack two weeks before the second meeting at the Pit, hounded and threatened by the KGB. I remember Ovsishcher and Al'shansky , who had already been demoted to the ranks, speaking at the meetings, shouting over the loudspeakers.

There were no barricades or trenches there, but in every sense, Jewish people and the KGB were on opposite sides of the invisible barricades.

People descending into the Pit (photo by Hanoh Feldman)

We, the people, walked between two rows of KGB men, policemen, and also the volunteers who helped the police for a couple of extra vacation days, like the old Jews in the center of this picture.

There was a meeting where one of the speakers—jokesters called people like him "well-trained Jews"—was declaring that our road was with the Communist Party, with the Soviet people. I had nothing against good people who happened to live in the Soviet Union, but at that time, I already fully understood that my road was very different from the one plowed by the Communist Party. Our roads formally diverged later, in 1988.

The Pit looks very different these days. In 2000, a touching monument was added, representing a group of haggard victims

Monument in the Pit

descending to their deaths into the Pit. It was created by the
Belarusian artist Leonid Levin and the Israeli sculptor Elsa
Pollak. It has been a target of vandalism, since even dead Jews
bother some people, but it still stands tall.

Now in Minsk there is also a very moving memorial to the
German and Austrian Jews killed in the ghetto—an empty,
broken dinner table and a lone chair. There is a small but
active Jewish community in Minsk these days, the synagogues
function, matzah is baked for Passover. *Am Israel Chai*—despite
everything, the people of Israel live!

CHAPTER 39

Our First Attempt To Emigrate

We got our first apartment in 1977, and I described how I was trying to furnish and improve it and how we were planning to live there for many years. This euphoria lasted for two years, and then we suddenly woke up. We despised the authoritarian regime we had to live with, were very unhappy with our jobs, and saw how anti-Semitism was affecting our daughter. Still, each of us had to overcome some obstacles to come to the decision to emigrate. For Boris, it was finishing one paper after another; for me, it was the position of my only brother, who was very much against emigration. At that time, it meant that if we left, I would never see him and his family again.

We both became ripe for action only in 1979. By that time, we had already said goodbye at the railway station to two of my cousins and many other friends and relatives from Minsk. We were planning to emigrate together with my parents; Boris's parents were to follow.

At that moment, I was still trying to find a good desk lamp for Boris. When we decided to emigrate, I stopped decorating our apartment, and in the next nine years never bought the lamp.

To apply for emigration, we had to receive a formal invitation from a direct relative in Israel. My mother's real brother in Israel had already passed away. The invitations were supposed to come from my mom's nonexistent sister. This was common practice, since many archives were destroyed during the war and women did not have to have the same last names to be sisters. It was almost impossible for the authorities to prove that these fake sisters never existed.

We waited for the invitations for a very long time. They were hanging in some KGB purgatory for many months and arrived finally in the summer of 1980.

In the late seventies, in Minsk, there was a two-stage system of applying for immigration to Israel. First, people had to register for the wait list with the local OVIR (Office of Visas and Registration), and only when their turn came could they officially apply. Our turn was in November of 1980.

Jews had always been used as bargaining chips between the Soviet Union and the West. Whenever the Western countries "misbehaved," the Soviets would shut down Jewish emigration. When, in response to the Soviet invasion of Afghanistan, the Western governments announced the boycott of the 1980 Summer Olympics in Moscow, the emigration process stopped. We couldn't apply, couldn't even officially become refuseniks, since in Minsk they introduced the requirement of all close relatives applying together. My brother didn't want to emigrate, and hiding his existence was impossible.

Boris was upset but continued doing his math. I was devastated. Each day, I would come from work and do something I had never done either before or after; I would play solitaire, always asking the same question: "When are we going to leave?" The answer was always very depressing—you will leave but many years later. Somehow, the cards knew the truth.

Me being me, I blamed myself for not applying earlier, for not pushing Boris to do something to speed up the process while it was still possible.

Whatever happens in people's lives, eventually they adjust. Of course, I adjusted too. Life went on. At the beginning of 1985, I became pregnant with our second child.

As I mentioned before, my dad died unexpectedly when I was eight months pregnant with Irina. I was always very close to Dad. Since I had some health problems, my ob-gyn told Boris to hide this news from me. With us having lived in Minsk for so many years, the only way to keep me from learning was to make sure that I didn't accidentally run into anyone who knew what happened. Under false pretenses, I was put in a hospital and stayed there until Irina's birth. I never said goodbye to my dad and did not attend his funeral.

Our younger daughter Irina was born in October of 1985. Another detail, describing Soviet medical care: She was born at four in the morning. When I was brought into the delivery room, I was the only patient, and the midwife and the nurses hated me; I ruined their attempt to sleep. They were extremely rude with me, screamed at me, but I was concentrating on one thing only—giving birth to a healthy baby. My baby was indeed perfect, and even the usually unfriendly nursing assistants gave her the affectionate nickname Thumbelina.

My baby Irina

To me, Irina's birth was a justification of our not emigrating earlier. I was holding in my hands my perfect baby and thought that it was meant to be. I didn't want another baby born in another place; I wanted this one and felt so lucky to have her.

I learned about Dad's death after having been back home with Irina for one very happy week. That same night I developed a 105-degree fever, an infection, and eventually had to have four surgeries, three of them done without any anesthesia. I also had to take my mom in to live with us, and after Dad's sudden death, Mom became delusional and very aggressive. Antidepressants were not available, and I remember happily spending the early morning hours with Irina and waiting with fear for Mom's door to open. It was very hard to see my mom in this angry woman who blamed everyone for Dad's death. I understood that it wasn't her fault, but it took me many years to restore in my memory the image of my loving mom, to start seeing happy dreams about her.

Irina was a very active child. Fortunately, at that time, women like me had a choice of staying home to care for the new baby for two years, a big part of it without pay. We jumped at this opportunity.

I don't know how I would have survived without it and without the help of thirteen-year-old Lena. Our friends called her Deputy Mom and they were right. While going through the surgeries, I had to spend time with the baby, hunt for groceries, prepare food for all five of us, clean and do our laundry, take care of Mom, and several months later move from our apartment to a new and bigger one, the result of exchanging ours and my parents' apartment for one. Mom could not live alone; it was obvious to everyone.

Though by Soviet standards it was a very good apartment, I never learned to like it. When I think about "my apartment" in Minsk, I always see our earlier place on Vostochnaya Street and my first attempts to decorate my own home.

CHAPTER 40

Chernobyl

On April 26, 1986, the Chernobyl nuclear disaster occurred. About 70 percent of the radioactive fallout landed in Belarus, and one-fourth of its territory was heavily contaminated. Minsk was located approximately two hundred miles north of Chernobyl, and some areas around the city were also affected.

Trying to cover up the truth, the government withheld information from its own people. The first of May was a national holiday, and many of Boris's colleagues went to villages close to Chernobyl to help their relatives plant potatoes and other vegetables. In the coming years, most of them died from cancer.

My cousin, a healthy and happy mother of two children, got caught in the radioactive rain one of the first few days after the accident. She lived in Gomel, only eighty miles from Chernobyl. Six months later, she died from leukemia.

We were lucky; we found out about the accident earlier than most people. The radioactive cloud reached Sweden; otherwise, the world and the Soviet people would have never known about the Chernobyl disaster. The sister of our very close friend was living in the United States. She called and warned all of us to stay inside. Before this call, I was spending a lot of time outside with our six-month-old Irina.

Of course, we could not stay inside forever. We also had no way to check if the food we were buying in the stores or at the farmers market was relatively clean. One of the first actions of the Soviet government was to confiscate all the Geiger counters used for detecting and measuring radiation.

At the same time, Boris's institute began distributing small plots of land for building dachas, tiny summer cottages—a dream of every Soviet citizen. One lab at the institute still had a Geiger counter, necessary for their work. People from this lab inspected the land and deemed it clean. We knew nothing about agriculture, but our idea was to grow clean produce for our children.

Our plot of land was actually a forest. With the help of our friends, Boris uprooted the trees and together they built a tiny shed, where we could store our shovels and rakes and hide from the rain. To reach it, we had to walk almost an hour from the train station to the plot and an hour back, and the trip back sometimes involved carrying a potato sack. The land was virgin and, as such, very productive, and without any knowledge, we managed to have a pretty good crop. We knew that body weight mattered and babies were especially vulnerable to radiation. Mostly, we were growing root vegetables. We found storage for them in the village, and these vegetables lasted for our Lena until New Year and for Irina until May. We also grew fruits and berries, and I cooked jams and different fruit preserves for the winter.

My father-in-law was a war veteran and thus had to wait for "only" ten years to buy a car. Fortunately, by that time, he was first on the wait list. We gave him all our savings; he added some, bought a small Russian-made Zhiguli sedan, and made it a gift to us.

It took a couple years to get a place in some far-from-home garage, so for the first several nights, Boris slept inside this car. He was very afraid that someone would steal this treasure. Eventually, he calmed down. When parking on the street, people always took care to take home everything easily removable—the windshield wipers and the mirrors—lest they be stolen. Foreign visitors were invariably amused by this. One of our friends always took his ancient car's battery home with him in the winter to keep it warm; otherwise, his car wouldn't start. Finding replacement parts was extremely difficult.

Boris has many other talents, but he was not natural at driving. His instructor, a Jewish refusenik who couldn't find another job, told Boris that he was his worst student ever. Boris didn't get discouraged; his goal was to learn to drive to the dacha and back. Eventually, he managed, and it made our lives easier.

After Chernobyl, I stopped giving Irina fresh milk. On each business trip to Moscow, Boris would buy Finnish dry milk, which was impossible to find in Minsk. My poor baby only tried fresh milk again two years later in Vienna.

When Boris grew more comfortable with driving, we often went to Vilnius. Lithuania was better supplied and much less affected by Chernobyl, so we brought home groceries for the whole family.

Until we emigrated, each time I cooked food for my family, I was wondering whether I was nourishing or poisoning them. We heard the rumors that every surgery department in every hospital in Minsk had turned into an oncology center but had no means of verifying or disproving them. My worries were all about my children.

CHAPTER 41

Boris's Career In The Soviet Union

Boris worked at the aforementioned Research Institute of Land Reclamation and Water Management for sixteen years, from 1973 until our departure from the Soviet Union in 1988. He was developing mathematical models for some diffusion and control problems related to the groundwater regime of the soil. He got two patents without any coauthors and was a good employee.

At the same time, he used every free minute at work and all evenings and weekends to do his beloved mathematics. It was a huge sacrifice on his side and, in many aspects, an even bigger one on mine. In one year, he wrote his PhD thesis while working this way, and the defense committee, which often did not look favorably at Jewish applicants, voted for him unanimously. By the time of his thesis defense, Boris was twenty-five, and he continued working thereafter in the same mode but with increased tempo and dedication.

To publish each paper, Boris had to get permission from the head of his lab and then from a so-called "expert committee." He had to approach the members individually and beg for their signatures. These "experts" understood nothing of his mathematics, so he had to rely mostly on his charisma and personal relationships. His boss, of course, was listed as the coauthor on all the papers related to melioration; otherwise, he would not have signed the permission slips.

When all the "experts" signed off, he had to get a signature from the institute director or one of his deputies. The director was very anti-Semitic, so his approval was out of the question. Every time, Boris had to wait until the director was on one of his business trips; only then could he go to the more sympathetic deputy director and get the coveted signature. The amount of time and energy required to get permission to publish a paper was probably equal to that required to actually write it.

This situation was not unique to Boris. One of our university classmates, who was one of the four Jews "distributed" with me to the Academy of Sciences and who shared my fate, also ended up in a place that had nothing to do with mathematics. Many years later, we met him at a conference in Sicily. Boris and I spent an evening with him. When he told us about the humiliation he had to go through while attempting to publish his papers, I could barely hide my tears. I do not know what made me cry—his quiet nontheatrical manner, his stuttering, or that I was just reliving our past.

The ideal work for a researcher was either in one of the research institutes at the Academy of Sciences or in a university or many other educational institutions. During these years, Boris made several attempts to change his job, and each time he failed.

Once, when in order to avoid hiring Boris, the personnel department violated the existing law, Boris confronted the dean of the College of Engineering. His response was, "Go and work where they are still keeping you!" Ironically, several months later, this man was awarded the Order of Friendship of Peoples.

In some perverted sense, this dean was right—keeping Boris's current job was also not a simple task. His institute's director was a zoological anti-Semite, and during his tenure, he fired almost all Jewish employees. With all his accomplishments, Boris literally hung by a thread.

Each trip to a domestic conference was preceded by a battle. Each invitation to a conference abroad went directly into a drawer in Boris's desk—there was never any hope of getting the KGB's permission to attend.

In the United States, there is only one scientific doctoral degree, called PhD. In the Soviet Union, like in many European countries, there existed a second, much higher degree, called Doctor of Sciences—equivalent to a habilitation in Europe. By the mid-eighties, Boris had many papers, had a monograph published by the best scientific publisher in Moscow, was well-known in the West, and had his doctoral dissertation ready. He had everything but the hope of being able to defend it.

Then, at a conference, Boris met Professor Yuri Mikhailovich Ermoliev who held research positions not only in Kiev but also at IIASA, the International Institute of Applied Systems Analysis in Vienna, Austria. He told Boris that his Western colleagues in Vienna spoke highly of him and asked him why he had not yet defended his doctoral thesis. After Boris's explanation, his first question was, "So, are you officially a Jew?" After getting the affirmative reply, Ermoliev thought for a while and then said, "We will do it in Kiev, at the Institute of Cybernetics of the Ukrainian Academy of Sciences."

It was a huge victory for Boris. He got very nice reviews and went through a very important process called pre-defense, after which the positive outcome of the defense itself was more or less assured. By that time, something was starting to happen in the country.

CHAPTER 42

Our Second Attempt

At the end of 1987, perestroika was gaining steam. We started hearing rumors that the authorities had lifted the requirement of all direct relatives emigrating together. This time, we decided to apply for the permission to emigrate on the first day it became possible.

Boris's doctoral defense was scheduled in Kiev for January 29, 1988. After some hard thinking, I became convinced that proceeding with it would be morally wrong. It would certainly cause trouble for those who had accepted him for doctoral defense, since he was not just a Jew but a Jew who was going to leave his homeland. They would never do it again for another Jewish person.

It was not easy to convince Boris to cancel his defense. I cannot blame him—he worked so hard to reach this point. He had not only spent years writing his dissertation, but he had also struggled for years to find a scientific council willing to accept his work. When we look back, we both know that he did the right thing when he finally agreed with me, but even now, almost thirty-five years later, he still sometimes reminds me that I robbed him of this moment of glory.

In 2021, Boris was elected a Foreign Member of Ukraine's National Academy of Sciences, which, I hope, should alleviate some of his old pain. It is also one more refutation of Putin's lie which describes Ukraine as a Nazi state. He was elected by secret ballot, though his last name and appearance are unmistakably Jewish.

Anyway, in January of 1988, Boris agreed to cancel his defense, and that was our Rubicon; there was no way back after it.

We were ready, but still couldn't receive even one official invitation from Israel. Our names were on every list possible, and we checked our mail with new hope every day, but nothing was there. Our hands were tied; invitations were required.

The original plan was to leave together with Boris's parents and my mom. Mom first agreed to it, but then she changed her mind. My brother was staying, and at that moment, his influence was much stronger than mine. And the invitations were now supposed to come from my mother-in-law's nonexistent sister.

At that time, Israel didn't have diplomatic relations with the Soviet Union. The Soviet government had severed them in 1967, and they were only reestablished in 1991, right after the Soviet Union's collapse. Desperate, Boris went to Moscow in the hope that the Dutch embassy, which was then representing Israeli interests in the Soviet Union, would be able to help us. Of course, it was very naive—in reality, he was not able to get into the embassy at all. Boris always remembered this day as one of the most miserable days of his life. It was January 29, the very day when he was supposed to have been in Kiev becoming a Doctor of Sciences.

Portrait by street artist of Borya

A street artist captured the intensity, the sadness, and the determination in Boris's face. Boris walked into the Central Post Office and phoned our only close friends in America—Galina and Vladimir Landres—asking if they could somehow help us. The answer was yes, they could, and they would.

There was a company in the United States that dealt in such invitations. We had no idea about it at the time. Someone would pay for them in the United States, and the recipient in the Soviet Union would receive the necessary papers from Israel. Several years later, we used the same company to help my relatives in Baku.

In a week, we received the perfect invitation. It even stated the maiden name of the invitee, which corresponded to my mother-in-law's maiden name. Funny, but simultaneously we got probably fifteen other invitations from different women, all dated differently. The KGB had been holding them for all these long months.

From that moment, we began a bizarre game with the local OVIR. It was a strange time for them too, since the rules of the game were changing almost daily. We would call the OVIR one day, and they would tell us that, to apply, we had to live together with Boris's parents. We would start devising a grand scheme for exchanging the apartments, but then we would call OVIR again, just to check if anything had changed and, sure enough, a different requirement would already have replaced this one.

The most unusual thing happened when Boris was told that his parents could go, but we could not, since the aunt was not a direct relative to Boris, only to his mom. It seemed hopeless, but Boris's creative mind devised yet another scheme. He invented a daughter for his dad, whom the latter had supposedly fathered out of wedlock during the war and who had somehow ended up in Israel. This phantom daughter would be a sister to Boris; hence, we would also meet the requirements of reuniting with direct relatives.

It is funny (though only in retrospect), but it was extremely difficult to convince my father-in-law to cooperate. He was proper and honest to a fault, and even the thought of an illegitimate daughter repulsed him. Fortunately, my mother-in-law always knew how to convince her husband. Happy, Boris called the OVIR for the fiftieth time. The man on the other end of the line told him not to worry—because OVIR had already lifted all the requirements anyway. We could come and bring all the documents to them.

The same day, we managed to find a typist specializing in such documents, and Boris spent the whole night dictating our data to her. We had to move quickly, since we could expect some new complications the next day. When the documents were ready, we had to do several more things, all quite painful. First, Boris and I had to put the official seals on our documents at our respective places of work, thus making our intent known to both human resources departments.

We could not afford the luxury of resigning. It was very unclear if we would get permission to emigrate in the end. We knew that many people who had emigrated before us had many unpleasant moments with their bosses and colleagues.

I was the first one to talk to my boss. I guess I was noticeably anxious because he looked at me and said, "Why are you so nervous? You are not going to hijack a plane, are you? You are not violating any laws." I was speechless. Then he offered me not to disclose anything to my colleagues, which surprised me even more but made me very happy. He spared me many unpleasant hours. When we finally got the permission to emigrate and I did resign, the reason for my resignation became widely known. Some people arranged a farewell party for me, but others immediately stopped talking to me. By then, I really could not care less.

Boris was not so lucky. He asked his head of Human Resources to keep his application secret. She promised, but within the hour, the whole institute knew that Boris was about to leave his homeland for the aggressive Zionist State of Israel. I will describe the consequences in the following chapter.

The last step was to let my brother know that we had made this decision and it was final. At that time, my brother did not consider emigration for himself and his family and did not approve of it. He was also very sad that we were splitting up our tight-knit family, since if successful, we would possibly never see each other again. We were so afraid of his reaction that we enlisted the help of my nephews—his sons—but he, though obviously very distraught, did not say any harsh words to us.

The invitation included my mom. She first agreed to go with us but then, after a conversation with my brother, firmly refused.

It was very painful for me. Of course, I knew that I really wanted to take my sick mom with us, and it was not my fault that she was staying. I also knew that I had obligations toward my children and my husband. Still, I was leaving my family, my mom.

On February 23, 1988, we officially applied for permission to leave the Soviet Union.

CHAPTER 43

How We Were Waiting

On the surface, my life didn't change much after we applied. I was still going to work every working day and was busy with my routine chores after work. Inside me, an invisible clock was ticking. It measured the time I had left to be with my mom, my siblings, my nephews, and my friends.

Boris had a much more eventful time at work. His director renewed his efforts to get rid of one of the very few Jews left at his institute. Being not very bright, he fired Boris for being overqualified.

To the Western reader, there is nothing strange about this formula, though people are usually not fired for being too good. In the Soviet Union, it was different. People were either fired (very rarely) for being extremely poor performers, for missing days or months of work, or sometimes because their positions had been liquidated. In some perverse sense, this director was ahead of his time.

Several months later, we discovered that firing Boris was just one part of his grand plan. Doing this to Boris was not enough for him. He also wrote to the KGB that a very talented mathematician was about to leave the Soviet Union, asking them to prevent this horrible brain drain. Again, this is another thing which is almost funny in retrospect, since this was the same director who had been trying to rid the institute of Boris for at least ten years. I am glad that the second part of his brilliant plan to finally destroy Boris was unknown to us at that time; we had enough problems with the first part.

Not only was Boris's salary essential to the well-being of our family but also, as I mentioned above, we didn't yet know if we would be allowed to leave at all. We were also certain that finding another professional job in the event of a refusal would be impossible. Ever the fighter, Boris started one more battle to save his job.

The uncertainty of the perestroika times helped him win. He went to see the district attorney and basically repeated the words of my boss, stating that he is being punished for acting in accordance with the laws of the country. Either the poorly stated reason for firing Boris had angered the district attorney, or perhaps there were orders to be nice to Jews for the time being, but he called the director an idiot and made a threatening call. Boris was reinstated.

Boris is forty

The frightened director allowed Boris to work until our departure. His mantra became "Don't touch Mordukhovich. There is a possibility of Zionist provocations."

On April 8, Boris turned forty. Big "0" birthdays are always emotional, but this one was especially touching. All our guests knew of our status, and there was such a mixture of emotions in the air—the hopes were intermixed with sadness. We hoped to build a new life elsewhere, but what about here? We were leaving so many people behind. I wrote a poem dedicated to Boris, which Lena sang beautifully to her own music. In that poem, I compared Boris to a horseman riding his horse too hard. Now his horse was sick; it was limping. The horseman himself was very tired, but he would never stop. He was getting ready for a really big jump, and I was asking him to take me with him but to be gentle with his horse and with me too.

Our friends produced a book titled *Boris Mordukhovich in the Memories of His Contemporaries.* Lena and I contributed to it too. Boris always was and still is a good source of funny stories, and to his credit, he always tolerated the jokes about himself very well and laughed with the rest of us. Most of the "authors" at that time had no definite plans to emigrate. Fortunately for us, most of them now live "on our shore." I am happy to say that we already have volumes 2 and 3 published, using a bit more sophisticated equipment, and the list of authors is growing. Hopefully, one day, a new volume will include stories written by our grandchildren.

By mid-May, there was a big change in our mood. People who had applied much later than we did were already being granted permission to leave. At first, we thought it was just a minor delay, but then it became more and more obvious that our file was given special, more serious consideration. We knew that the OVIR was just a front for the KGB, but we could speak only with them. Soon, we started visiting the OVIR every Friday, asking if any decision had been made. We even devised our own little strategy: We would both come to the OVIR together and check to see which of the two clerks was sitting at the front desk—the man or the woman. The man seemed a little friendlier with me, while the woman was a bit nicer with Boris. Nice or not, each time we were getting no answer.

We were advised to wait patiently, but we decided to disregard this advice. All other applicants were communicating with their district or city OVIRs. Boris went further, to the Republican OVIR. The man in charge of it belonged to a new generation of Soviet bureaucrats. In his mid-thirties, he called himself a "Gorbachev man." In contrast to his subordinates at the city OVIR, he was polite and even seemed sympathetic. Still, the visits to him led nowhere.

We were getting more and more anxious. From our past experiences, we knew that the short window of opportunity could be closed at any minute. The gossip mill was working at full speed, and all the rumours were pessimistic. We fully realized that it would be horrible to remain in the Soviet Union, especially as people who had once applied for emigration, as refuseniks. Boris became a regular at the Republican OVIR, but to no avail.

One day, Boris received an unexpected call from the "Gorbachev man." He asked Boris to come to his office immediately. When Boris entered the room, very familiar to him by now, he was surprised to see the head of the office sitting in the corner. In his place at the big desk sat a general in the uniform of the Internal Troops of the Ministry of Internal Affairs, obviously waiting for Boris. He introduced himself as the deputy minister of Internal Affairs of Belarus. The general told Boris that his ministry had received a signal that Boris was an outstanding mathematician. The general apologized for all the injustice that Boris had experienced for many years and offered him a chair position at the university.

He assured Boris that everything had already been approved by the president of the Academy of Sciences of Belarus, Vladimir Petrovich Platonov. This story was corroborated many years later by Platonov, whom Boris knew well.

Boris kept his cool and replied to the general that he, Boris, would love to stay, but his mom was adamant, and he had to leave with his mother. It was a lie, of course, but they couldn't fire his mom; she wasn't working anyway. The general gave Boris the word of honor that he would be able to visit his mom in Israel whenever he wished. Boris replied that he completely trusts the general, but someday, there might be another deputy minister who might look at things differently. Boris's reply was a polite "No." It was a game, and the general understood it perfectly. He told Boris that, since he wasn't able to convince him to stay, we should get a permission to leave very soon.

Now, looking back, I realize that our entire saga lasted less than six months, nothing in comparison with the plight of the refuseniks of the seventies. Still, since all our friends and acquaintances were getting permissions in two months, we were very alarmed by the delay and even more by the offers to stay.

After the meeting with the general, Boris started calling the head of the Republican OVIR even more often. One of the signs of the new times was the patience of the Gorbachev bureaucrat. He tried to calm Boris down. When Boris finally told him that if we didn't receive a reply in several days, we'd call the foreign press and start a hunger strike, his partner-in-conversation confessed that the decision-maker (a KGB man) was fishing at that time and asked Boris to wait just a couple more days. By doing this, he actually admitted that he, the head of the Republican (Belarusian) OVIR, was just a pawn, and that all the decisions were made behind the scenes by someone really powerful, thus revealing the "secret de Polichinelle."

Finally, when Boris called the Republican OVIR one more time, he was advised to open a bottle of champagne—the permission was granted. We ran with Lena to a small café in a nearby park, and celebrated, just the three of us, by ordering ice cream.

Our Lena still remembers how, when Boris went to the restroom, the waiter tried to kick the two of us out of the restaurant, assuming that we were there to pick up men. We were dressed modestly, didn't even wear any makeup, but we were two women sitting at the table without a man. She also remembers how I told her to memorize the way ordinary people were treated in that country.

A couple of days later, Boris and I were already in Moscow. This time, we were able to enter the Dutch consulate. We received the Israeli visas there, and then ran to the Austrian embassy to get the Austrian visas. When all the necessary documents were in my purse, we called my brother's home and Boris proudly told my nephew Leo, "We are already Americans!" He was a little wrong. We were not Americans just yet.

CHAPTER 44

Departure

The time between that day and our departure is one big blur. We had so much to do.

We could not sell our apartment; we had to leave it behind. The challenge was to make my mom its owner; otherwise, the government would take it away, moving my mom into some studio instead. I wanted the family of my brother to be able to use it after we were gone. It was very difficult to accomplish, but Boris rose to the challenge, and we had fewer crystal vases to worry about.

Then we had to renounce our Soviet citizenship formally and pay 700 rubles each to the state, a total of 2,800 rubles for all of us—twenty times the average monthly salary of an average Soviet citizen at that time. This included having to renounce Lena's passport. She had just turned sixteen and did not have a passport yet, so we had to formally obtain her passport and then give it up, paying the required extra 700 rubles in the process. We had to buy expensive tickets to Vienna and some presentable clothes to last us until we would be able to find jobs. We had to buy canned food to take with us to supplement the allowance we would get on the way to America. For the same purpose, most immigrants bought some things to sell in Austria and Italy. Following this advice, we got into serious trouble later.

Someone advised us to buy the warmest down comforters, since it might get cold while we were in transit in Italy. This was the best advice we got. These comforters saved us later, and I called them our comrades in emigration.

To get money for all this, we had to sell our furniture, our car, and our books. Selling books was very painful, and I would never have agreed to it if only we had been able to take them with us. I remembered where I bought each book, when I read it for the first time, and which emotion it evoked in me. I felt like I was betraying my best friends. Unfortunately, the law did not permit us to take any serial editions, older books, or books with handwritten notes. Boris could not even take his published papers, to say nothing of preprints. In the end, he sent them through the Dutch embassy to Israel, and retrieved them several years later when he visited Israel for the first time.

At times, I felt lost. I had the two-year-old Irina and my sick mom on my hands. Boris was handling the sale of the car, and I was taking care of the rest. I was also dealing with my guilt of leaving my mom behind. I would never have accomplished

With my kids

anything in such a short time if it were not for Lena.

She took care of Irina when we had to go to Moscow for visas and on many other occasions. She was with me when a man who behaved very much like a sex maniac came to buy our books. Our door was always open to potential buyers, and I had never held such a large sum of cash before or since. I kept it in a purse and constantly kept losing it. "Where is my silver purse?" was my mantra those days.

Lena and her best school friend Alla Bogina helped pack our suitcases, with Alla often deciding what we needed and what we did not need on this journey. I was extremely grateful for it, for I was overwhelmed and appreciated any advice. We could take with us two suitcases per person. We had to pack canned food, pots and pans, down blankets and bedding, summer and warm clothing for everyone. The crown jewel of this collection was Irina's chamber pot.

Boris and I took our already sold car on its last trip. We made a sentimental journey, saying goodbye to Russia. We visited mostly the towns of the so-called Golden Ring, famous for their beautiful churches. One of the nights on this trip was unforgettable.

We arrived in the town of Ivanovo late in the evening, very tired from many days on the road. This was a town famous for its textile industry, where mostly women worked. We saw very few men on the streets, but everyone we saw was visibly drunk. Sleeping in the car seemed dangerous. At that time, every hotel in the Soviet Union required potential guests who wanted to share a room to present their passports as proof that they were legally married. Our Soviet passports had already been taken away from us. To get into a hotel people needed a passport. Boris had with him the passport of our friend Misha Dubov, who didn't look like him but also had a beard, whereas I did not have any ID whatsoever. In most places, Boris just shamelessly bribed the women at the reception with smoked sausage and other goods, but in Ivanovo, for some reason, it did not work. We drove from one hotel to another, until finally, a kind receptionist explained to Boris that police officers were frequently checking their hotel, arresting the prostitutes with their clients. I was staying in the car all the time, so I was not offended, just exhausted.

There was only one room available. Boris was ready for desperate measures. He offered to show the woman our Israeli visas as proof of our legal marital status, and she agreed. Happy, he ran to the car to update me on the good news. Then he opened the folder where our visas were supposed to be . . . and they were not there.

Since I knew that Boris handled the visas last, I literally put my hand over my mouth to refrain from saying everything I meant to say. Boris was circling the car, looking desperate, when all of a sudden he burst out laughing.

This is when I graduated from being scared to being terrified. Here I was, in some godforsaken place, ten days before our departure, and not only had our visas disappeared but also my husband had just lost his mind. I carefully approached Boris, trying not to aggravate his condition.

As it happened, he did not go crazy after all. Boris was a big fan of Dale Carnegie's books, which we read in the samizdat version. In particular, he liked the idea that in the most horrible situations, a person had to imagine the worst possible scenario and then accept it. He imagined us coming to the OVIR to see the same people, whom we had visited every Friday for several months, and announcing "We lost our visas. Let's start it all over again."

I was not amused. Boris took me to the railway station, where he found a stationary sleeping car and a woman willing to let us sleep in an empty compartment for ten rubles. I was sure she took me for Boris's lover, or, much worse, one of the ladies of the night who were frequenting the railway station area, but at that moment, I didn't care. Boris fell asleep momentarily, and I was listening to his even breathing all this long, sleepless night. In the morning, we started calling every place we visited on this trip, and lo and behold, we found our visas. Boris left them at the Red Cross Office in Moscow. We had gone there to document that my dad was buried in Minsk. If regular visits to the Soviet Union remained impossible, the Red Cross could help me visit his grave. We returned home to Minsk two days later with our visas intact.

I cannot describe my last week in Minsk. How do you leave forever your mother, your brother, your friends, everything that was dear to you, and stay sane? I do not know if everyone felt the same way, but I certainly did. How do you leave behind everything you worked so hard for and start a new life from scratch at forty? This was an easier question for me. You work hard and build this new life and a new home for your children. Things could be replaced, but people, people . . .

I will never forget the railway station, where more than 150 people gathered to say goodbye to us. My brother Boris was crying as if he were at my funeral. Wherever I looked, I saw familiar faces. I knew that I might never see them again.

Lena's friends brought her a huge teddy bear, which later became an object of very serious attention at customs. I remember holding Irina's little hand very tight, like it was a lifeline.

Four of our close friends accompanied us on the first leg

Picture from my exit visa

of this journey. We went together by train to Brest, a city on the Soviet-Polish border. When we arrived there, I was so exhausted that one of the friends had to help me spell my name in Russian, letter by letter.

We did not carry anything prohibited, but I knew that they took many people for a personal search and even a gynecological exam, and I was very afraid of such humiliation. I vividly remember my fear that any nonentity in uniform could degrade me, insult me, and I would not be able to protect that which was inconspicuous but incredibly important to me—sorry for big words—my dignity.

Fortunately, the screeners were mostly busy with Lena's bear, suspecting that it was full of diamonds. They did not search either our luggage or us at all. We were lucky; the bear proved to be innocent, and we were let go.

The suspected ursine smuggler is aging well. After more than thirty-five years of moving from one country to another, from one city to a different one, he still looks young and handsome.

We waved to our friends and formally crossed the border, as we thought, forever. To the vast amusement of other emigrants, Irina staged a small political manifestation, proclaiming that she did not want to leave. Everyone, including us, burst into nervous, almost hysterical laughter.

Finally, we boarded the train. Our route went through Warsaw and Prague to Vienna.

CHAPTER 45

Vienna

When we finally arrived in Vienna, representatives of the two agencies met us at the railway station. Those going to Israel were quickly led away by people from Sochnut, the Jewish Agency for Israel.

We, and several other families, who expressed the desire to go to the United States, were put on a small bus by a representative of the Hebrew Immigrant Aid Society (HIAS) and driven to a small hotel on Blumauergasse. We were assigned two rooms, one for our family of four and one for Boris's parents.

This was the first Western city in our lives. My initial impressions of it are still very clear in my mind. Of course, being from the Soviet Union, I looked with wide eyes at the selection of goods in the stores. I was awed by the assortment of different products, by the elegance of the clothing, by the jewelry in the store windows, by all the glitz. I cannot honestly call it window-shopping. I knew that I could not afford any of this, and it was fine with me. We were free, and that was the main thing.

The Blumauergasse is close to a huge entertainment park, Grabben, and to a red-light district. Fortunately, we also found ourselves within walking distance of the old city. It was very important, since we could not afford to use public transportation. Our Irina, who was not three yet, was very stubborn. She almost never allowed us to carry her. While we were exploring beautiful old Vienna, she accompanied us for hours on her small feet.

Once, in the evening, when Boris and I went for a walk, we saw a man taking money from the wall. Boris asked me what he was doing. I remembered something from reading many novels and guessed that he probably had a Visa (I meant a Visa card). Boris replied that we also have an Israeli visa and asked if we could get some money too. Our ignorance of the Western style of life was astonishing.

We were getting an allowance from HIAS, and in Vienna, HIAS paid for our accommodations. Like everyone else who left the USSR in those years, we had very limited funds: approximately 100 dollars per person. Hence, 400 dollars for our small family of four. Our team (two children and two aging parents) placed a huge responsibility on us. People who emigrated young and unencumbered probably do not even understand how much this responsibility affected us. Emigrants, according to—as it turned out—quite justified rumors, had a hard time in Italy, and most people brought with them some things for sale. It was a very strange assortment, from wind-up toys to expensive photo cameras, from linen bedding to—in our case—beautiful Baltic engravings. I later hid these engravings from Boris, realizing in time that we would still have another, American life. Now they decorate the walls of my study where I am writing this book.

Most people were selling things, thus supplementing their allowance, but some people were better at it than others. I must say that if, God forbid, we had to earn a living by trading, then even Boris would be a failure, but I would certainly be poorer than the proverbial church mouse.

Back in the Soviet Union, someone advised us to buy linens, photo cameras, and Cuban cigars for this purpose. Later, we sold most of our stuff cheaply to resellers, but on our first walk in Vienna, we had no idea that the resellers even existed. We observed that Cuban cigars were very expensive and decided to offer ours to tobacco shop owners for a very low price.

We spoke with several owners who all politely declined. No one told us that there was a state monopoly on the sale of tobacco products and that we were breaking the law. We would never violate any law on purpose, but "the ignorance of the law excuses no man."

Finally, Boris entered one more tobacconist, and the owner was interested. He suggested coming back the next morning at nine and bringing all the cigars we had.

The next day, we came together to the store entrance with all our cigars. Then I got one of my premonitions, which I can never explain but which are always worth listening to. I told Boris to enter the store with only one box. He looked at me as if I was crazy but agreed.

Further events developed as in a bad detective story. The friendly owner invited Boris to come into the inner room, where two police officers were waiting for him. The second day of our new life began in the most unusual way: I suddenly saw my handcuffed husband being taken out of the store by two police officers and led off to a police car. Fortunately, the tobacconist never saw me and did not know that Boris had an accomplice. We could not even say goodbye to each other, because the rest of the boxes were in a big black bag in my hands. One of the officers gave me a suspicious look, but the law did not allow him to search a random woman without any reason.

I remember the overwhelming feeling of despair. We managed to get out of the Soviet Union, and in one day ruined everything. My imagination was running wild, and all the scenarios in my head were horrifying. I was sure they would keep Boris in prison for years, and the rest of us would either be sent back to the Soviet Union or I would be arrested as an accomplice, and our children would be sent to an orphanage. Even when they would finally release Boris from prison, no country would ever accept us.

I had no idea how to get rid of the remaining boxes. I would have been happy to throw them into the river or the nearest garbage can, but I was afraid that someone would notice and report me to the police. I knew that the police might come to our hotel and search our room. Shivering from nerves on this warm September day, I was stumbling in the general direction of our hotel, clearly aware that I could not go there. Then I fortunately ran into Lena and my mother-in-law.

Lena, then sixteen, was our main comrade in arms during emigration. I took her aside and gave her an update on what had happened, warning her not to alarm the grandparents until necessary. We agreed that I would sit in a small park nearby, and she would keep me updated on what was going on in our hotel. I was sitting there thinking the eternal thoughts of many Jewish mothers before me: "What will happen to my children?"

Meanwhile, the police officers brought Boris to jail, undressed him, gave him a jail robe, and only then took him to a formal interview. Boris's command of the English language was very limited at that time, and these Austrian officers were not too proficient in English either. It still seems like an unbelievable miracle to me that he somehow managed to convey his story and even evoke their sympathy. They called the tobacco shop owner a jerk, returned Boris's clothes to him, and drove with him to Blumauergasse to confirm his story.

The officers were good men, and when they saw frightened children, old people with confused eyes, and our poverty, they became convinced that they were not dealing with a smuggler. They did not even search our room, but since the call from the shop owner was officially registered, the best they could do for Boris was to write that he had one pack of cigars too many in his luggage and to fine him the equivalent of 300 dollars, three-quarters of what we had. They assured Boris they would report nothing to HIAS. Boris paid his fine. The officers filled in all the necessary forms and left. Lena ran to the park to let me know that I could go home.

This story became folklore among Russian émigrés. We heard several narratives about this one moron who attempted to sell cigars directly to a tobacco shop owner. The moron and his wife were very modest and never confessed.

This incident was a huge shock to all of us but especially to my father-in-law. He was a very straitlaced man, and the thought of his son being arrested made him physically sick. Boris was very upset with the loss of the money. I was the only one who was extremely happy with the outcome, since my worst nightmares did not come true. I kept repeating to Boris that we would survive, but his brain was already working in a different direction

Since selling things was obviously not his forte, Boris decided to just walk into the Department of Mathematics at the University of Vienna, introduce himself, and offer to give a lecture. Now, after hundreds of lectures he gave all over the world, Boris still does not have any explanation for the informal treatment he got there.

With his Russian monograph in hand, Boris approached a group of professors and made his offer. One of the professors immediately invited him to give a talk at his seminar the next week. Then, to Boris's amazement, he opened his own wallet and gave Boris the equivalent of 100 dollars as an honorarium. There were no forms to fill out.

We were amazed by how informally things were done in the West. Now we know better. This kind man probably knew the plight of the Russian refugees, easily recognized Boris as one of them, and wanted to help.

I accompanied Boris to this lecture, which probably broke the world record for the number of English-language mistakes. My role was to make a list of all of them. Several attendees listened with interest and applauded at the end. After the lecture, the same professor invited us to a Viennese café for a treat, which was a major event for us. Oh, my first cappuccino, I shall never forget you!

Inspired, Boris gave one more lecture in Vienna, but no one gave him any money there. It did not discourage him, and later, in Italy, he lectured a couple more times. It did not make us rich, but gave him some experience and helped us survive.

The story of the tobacco shop owner has a continuation. I always remembered where the tobacco shop stood but was afraid of a confrontation and pretended not to. Many years and many trips later, on one of his visits to Vienna, Boris suddenly recognized the familiar tobacco shop. Curious, he went inside and spoke with the new owner. She told him that the previous owner had retired, calling him Herr Doktor. "Why did you call him a doctor?" asked Boris. The woman explained that this man was a Doctor of Law and a prominent Nazi who had lost his license after 1945. When Boris came home, he proudly informed me that he was the last victim of the Second World War.

Necessity is a great teacher. I never spoke Yiddish much and never studied German. Nevertheless, when Lena and I went to a farmers market, I managed to buy groceries there, successfully conversing with Austrian farmers in some strange mix of languages.

I like Vienna a lot. I like its cafés, the St. Stephen's Cathedral, the musicians on the street corners, its opera house, its Ring, and even the horses near Hofburg. Some of these memories are from my later visits when I was no longer a poor refugee.

I have loved opera since my childhood. Of course, I could not miss the Vienna State Opera. We bought very cheap tickets, and after standing on my feet for three hours, I knew that it was worth going there. Since then, whenever I got to Vienna, I lured Boris to the Opera, by hook or by crook winning back the evening from mathematics and mathematicians, and every time it was wonderful.

Viennese museums have one free day each month, and we were lucky to be there on such a day. It was a very busy day for us, and since then, I have become a faithful admirer of Vienna's Kunsthistorisches Museum with its amazing Brueghel.

For the first time in our lives, we attended Yom Kippur services in Vienna. HIAS took us to the beautiful historical Stadttempel, the only one of Vienna's ninety-three synagogues that survived the last world war. It was not spared for its beauty; it just could not be destroyed without setting fire to the adjacent buildings to which it was attached. This service deeply touched me, and ever since, the Yom Kippur service has been my favorite.

In 1981, Palestinian Arab terrorists attacked this synagogue with machine guns and hand grenades during a bar mitzvah ceremony, murdering two people and injuring thirty. Since then, this synagogue has been heavily guarded, as are other

Synagogue in Vienna

European synagogues. It surprised me then. Now terrorism has come to American Jewish houses of prayer. The violence against Jews is increasing, and no one seems surprised by that.

From our first visit, I remember not only the beautiful sites, not only our freedom and our poverty, but also an extreme feeling of not belonging. I had never been paranoid and never saw anti-Semitism and xenophobia in everyone, but I had a good reason to feel that way in Vienna.

I remember how a huge German shepherd pinned my tiny, terrified Irina to the ground, and the woman owner did not even apologize, did not call the dog off; I had to push the dog off my baby while the woman just continued marching. My imagination immediately drew a black uniform and a holster on the belt.

Another woman hit the little daughter of our friends with a shopping cart in the grocery store—hit her hard. The girl began to cry, but the woman did not even raise an eyebrow. Attitudes toward children and the elderly are always a litmus test; my internal radar turned on and never turned off. Many years later, at a conference, Boris met one professor who, in response to Boris's question about anti-Semitism, replied, "We Austrians always were and still remain anti-Semites." Many people were looking down their noses at us. We were clean; we did not smell, did not beg, did not steal. We were just different, poor, and strange. I never experienced anything like that either in Italy or in the United States.

However, I also remember the kindness of the Austrian professor, the understanding and sympathy of the two police officers, and to me, those outweigh the bad memories. It is good for my soul to remember being stateless and poor. I know that there are good people everywhere. I like Vienna, my first Western city, a lot. It will always be full of bittersweet memories for me.

Further events developed as in a *bad detective story.*

CHAPTER 46

To Italy

I am writing this chapter while in Italy, thirty years after the described events. I walk for hours, admiring the medieval streets and old buildings, taking in the charming atmosphere of an old town. It is winter, and there are almost no tourists here in Padua. I enter beautiful churches, and my steps resonate loudly in a cold and empty space. I have a lot of time to think, and my memory takes me back, when I was in Italy in a completely different situation. Now, at the farmers market, they call me Signora Americana. I have a home, a job, citizenship, and money. I arrived here by plane. I am free to go whenever and wherever I please. In 1988, everything was very different.

On the day of our departure from Vienna, the HIAS bus drove us to the railway station. Soldiers with machine guns met us and led us into a separate room, where they were guarding us until it was time to leave. There were rumors about terrorist threats.

We had no idea that in the eighties, Islamic terrorism was a serious threat in Europe. In the Soviet Union, the information was always one-sided, and we never heard of the attack on a synagogue in Rome in 1982, where thirty-seven people were injured. To my innocent mind, the word *terrorists* seemed too dramatic, and the threat nonexistent. When a year later, already in America, someone began to terrorize the software company where I worked with phone calls, notifying them that there was a bomb hidden in the building, my British boss almost had to kick me outside. He, like all Brits, knew very well how buildings could be blown up. He knew, but to me these calls seemed like pranks in poor taste. I was not afraid of anything; I had a lot of work and was sorry to waste time waiting in the yard for police with dogs to declare yet another call an empty threat. Only September 11, 2001, finally cured me of my naivete.

Going back to that day in Vienna, I remember many little children crying. The adults looked tense, which had nothing to do with the terrorists; they were worried about the upcoming journey. Every family had many suitcases or huge bags, sometimes custom-made—two per person, containing all their worldly possessions.

After what seemed like an eternity, the time came to board the train. We were going to Rome, a step closer to our final destination. The carriage was full, and the only people there were Soviet emigrants. Soldiers were guarding it from both ends. There were six people in every compartment, so we had a whole compartment for our family. A very long night was ahead of us.

Irina needed some sleep, and I made room for her. By the time she settled in, everyone else was asleep too. All the upper berths were occupied by our luggage. There was no space left for me. I quietly exited the compartment and spent this long night in the corridor, near the window. As usual, even then, I spent a lot of time listening to the life stories of folks I saw for the first and last time in my life. Talking was therapeutic to people, and I understood that very well. Finally, everything became quiet, and I was alone. I was staring into the night, trying to foresee the future, thinking about the people I left behind, about our past, but mostly dedicating time to my favorite occupation—worrying.

I remember how I tried to make out the names of small stations flashing in the dark outside the window; I remember how the train flew into the tunnels and back out into the darkness with a roar. I didn't even want to sleep. It was one of the most memorable nights of my life. A night between countries, between lives. A night when I tried to calculate, to foresee, something and guessed nothing, not even that Italy would somehow become very special to me.

At last, it became not that dark anymore. There was some movement in our compartment, and I went in trying to catch some sleep.

None of us were prepared for what happened next. We were expecting to see the outskirts of Rome soon, but the train began to slow down and came to a stop. There was nothing in sight but trees and fields. A loud voice ordered us to leave the train immediately. There was a moment of short panic—many people, especially the older ones, were visibly scared for their possessions. Soon, a line of men formed, Boris and his father among them. They were unloading the suitcases and bags through the doors and windows. All of this was done under the watchful eye of the armed soldiers. As I found out later, the train stopped each time in a different place because of the threat of a terror attack. Finally, the train whistled and left. Someone led us to the buses parked not far away.

In the years that followed, I stayed in hundreds of hotels all over the world. Most of the time, I forget their names as soon as I leave, but I will always remember the Hotel Nordland, our first home in Rome. We were given a week there to adjust, fill in some forms, and, most importantly, find an apartment in Ladispoli, a small resort town near Rome, the only place where we were allowed to stay.

The first evening in Hotel Nordland is memorable to me because of an episode which I call "my big disillusionment." The hotel provided us with a full board. It was time for dinner, and the waiters brought a big tray with fresh rolls of bread. Immediately, some of my compatriots began pushing other people away with their elbows, trying to get more rolls for themselves and their families. Now I am older and, I hope, wiser, and I think that these people were just frantic, scared to death of the unknown, of what was ahead of them. At the time, though, I was very upset, telling Boris that if all of them were going to America, I don't care to go there—a very childish reaction indeed.

In my previous life, I had a naive notion that all Jewish emigrants must be well-educated and cultured people, leaving for the same ideological reasons as us—people with strong moral principles. My Italian experience taught me that Jews, like any other ethnic group, have their own crooks, jerks, and people with shaky moral values and, like everyone else, should not be judged only by their worst.

Nevertheless, we were in Rome. Of course, we could not afford to spend money on public transportation. Many fellow émigrés were riding buses without paying the fare. The idea was that nobody could make you pay the fine if you did not have any money. "They'll just call you *Russo idiota* and let you go," one young man with shifty eyes confidently told me. I had strong objections to being called a Russian idiot, so we walked everywhere. I can still close my eyes and walk in my mind from Hotel Nordland to Vatican City, to the Colosseum, to my favorite—the Spanish steps. The streets were full of unfamiliar noises and strange smells. They were bursting with life. I was oscillating between the joy of being there and the sad feeling that I did not belong there or anywhere else. Would I ever belong? Will I find a place that I will be able to call home?

I did not just refuse to ride any public transportation without tickets; I also never went to the flea market Mercato di Porta Portese, nicknamed Americana, where most immigrants went to sell whatever they brought with them from the Soviet Union. From great photo cameras to children's toys and even condoms (advertised as "*anti-bambino*"), Russians were selling all the imaginable things there. Locals were paying for bargains, but someone once paid Boris much more than he asked for a collection of small pins. The earth stands on the shoulders of kind people.

I did not try to avoid the unpleasant for me job of selling things at the flea market. After losing so much, I was just frantically trying to hold on to some normality. I regret it now; I would probably have some colorful stories to share.

At that time, one Russian-speaking woman was in charge of the flock of refugees at Hotel Nordland. She was married to an Italian, and we were supposed to call her Signora Eleonora. Signora Eleonora strongly disliked us, despised our Soviet clothes, our naive questions, and our anxiety. She was an overdressed, overweight lady in flashy jewelry who talked to people through the corner of her brightly-painted mouth, and she immensely enjoyed the power she had over everyone around.

As I mentioned before, our main task for the week was to find an affordable apartment in Ladispoli, a town on the Mediterranean Sea, twenty-two miles west of Rome. In Italy, I finally realized that we human beings can accomplish almost anything if our survival depends on it.

The town was small. Potential apartments were intercepted and rented for an additional fee by enterprising emigrant brokers. We had nothing to pay the brokers, and also, because of the same naivete, we did not want to deal with people who profited from their impoverished emigrant brothers. Boris and I firmly memorized two Italian expressions—"*Affitasi appartamento*?" and "*Quanta costa*?" which enabled us to ask if there was an apartment for rent and how much it cost. Thus armed, we knocked on many doors, talking mostly with our hands. This was okay, since the Italians did the same. They often replied to our first question with "*Adesso*?" which means "Now?" To our Russian ears, it sounded like "Odessa." Odessa was a city in southern Ukraine whose jovial inhabitants, as the rumor mill reported, did not enjoy a very good reputation in Ladispoli. We firmly denied being from Odessa, replying, "No, Minsk." This answer, from the hosts' point of view, was very cryptic. We plunged the Italians into amazement and deprived ourselves of any chance of success.

Finally, by some miracle we managed to find a property owner with some knowledge of English. I have had several job interviews in America. None of them were as long or as thorough as this one. Later I realized that he had a good reason to be extra cautious. He was trying to psychoanalyze us and to determine if we were going to sell his furniture or steal his pots and pans, as some of our fellow countrymen were doing.

The interview was a huge success. As a result, we became happy dwellers of a two-bedroom apartment with tiled floors, not far from the sea. The rent was steep, and we could barely afford it with the stipend we got for our living expenses from the HIAS. For the sustenance, we were seriously counting on the canned food we had brought with us from Minsk.

Several days later, the buses took us to Ladispoli. We were to spend three months there, the most surreal period of my life

CHAPTER 47

Ladispoli

In 1988, Ladispoli was the main transit point for Jewish immigrants on their way to the United States. After entering Italy, the refugees had to file a petition with the United States consulate for political asylum and wait for their decision.

The main square of Ladispoli had a fountain. This fountain was a meeting point, a place where we were supposed to gather every evening at 7:00 p.m. for the news and messages from HIAS. This is where the more experienced émigrés passed their infinite wisdom on to the newcomers. There we learned that at the local market you were supposed to bargain. We were told that the cheapest food was turkey wings, immediately christened by Russians "The Wings of the Soviets," the name of a popular soccer team. The most enterprising or the most optimistic Russians tried to sell some merchandise right there. They exhibited their meager goods for public inspection on the rim of the fountain. Since everyone brought pretty much the same things to sell in Italy, no one was buying.

The market was a place that I hated and loved at the same time. I disliked it because I loathed bargaining, was terrible at it, and knew that I always overpaid which, at that time, we could not really afford. I loved it because it provided free entertainment which Lena, who always accompanied me there, and I both thoroughly enjoyed.

Of course, in order to communicate, not only did the Russians learn some Italian words but the Italian merchants also picked up some Russian and often used it very bizarrely. I remember a handsome Italian lad who was screaming something like "*Appelsino, vitamine per bambini*" (oranges, vitamins for children) nonstop. The Russian word for orange phonetically sounds approximately like *apple-sin* and doesn't resemble the Italian word for orange at all. *Vitamine* was a real Italian word, though, and it was very close to the Russian term for vitamins.

The best scene we saw there involved a plump middle-aged Italian vendor who knew the Russian word for cow (*ko-ro-va*) but didn't know the word for calf. She jumped like crazy in front of a scared-looking customer, keeping her index fingers close to her head, just like small horns, and screamed "*piccola korova, piccola korova*" (small cow), pointing at the veal liver at her counter.

These three months in Ladispoli were not easy. For me, unlike for some of my acquaintances, this first visit did not become a "Roman Holiday." This is where our little Irina, barely three, got terrible food poisoning, most likely from spoiled canned meat. We brought canned goods with us because from the letters of the earlier emigrants we expected not to have enough money for food. The young Russian pediatrician volunteer did not have any medical instruments with him. He almost cried when, in an attempt to assist her, he damaged something in her throat, causing bleeding—he had a small child of his own. It was very scary—my baby had a very high fever and was vomiting blood. She recovered, but was becoming more and more difficult. The nervousness of adults always reflects on their children, and there was plenty of anxiety in our household.

On the last Sunday of each month, the Vatican museums had free admission. On a hot day in October, we all went to see these museums, and there my mother-in-law collapsed and was taken to a hospital with heart problems.

Boris's parents were agitated all the time. No one could blame them—it was hard to leave everything behind and start a new life at forty, but at sixty-five, it must have been frightening.

I heard about nervous breakdowns and heart attacks that occurred during this period. It did not happen to us, but for some reason we had suddenly switched our previous quite traditional roles. The most relaxed, very uncharacteristically, was Boris. He did not study English, did not even do his beloved math. He read books we could not find in the Soviet Union, and for the first and last time in his life, he spent a lot of time with Irina. Burdened with a sense of responsibility, I spent every free minute improving my not-so-horrible English and expanding my professional skills.

I recently watched a movie about defectors who fled the Soviet Union during the most difficult times. Unlike them, we left legally. We did not have to sail the sea in a fragile boat or hijack a plane. We did not show any heroism, and I do not want to dramatize anything. To some, the Italian period of emigration must have seemed like a great vacation, but I honestly write about myself and about my perception.

Amazingly, neither my emotions nor our poverty affected my feelings for Italy. Just the opposite; this is when I fell in love for life. It was an inexplicable and unexpected love for the country— for beautiful towns, old churches, ancient ruins, and warm people. It was also love for the music of their speech, for their gesticulation, for the construction worker singing "La Donna è Mobile" in an almost operatic voice, for the continuous theater which Italian street life is to me. It was love for its blue skies and narrow streets, for Piazza San Marco in Venice which I still see in my dreams, for everything that Italy was and still is to me.

None of us had Italian visas. With our semilegal status, we did not have permission to travel farther than Rome, but of course, we did. Some smart entrepreneur was running a cheap Russian tour company, and we were able to see Venice, Florence, San Marino, Naples, Capri, Pompeii, and Sorrento.

We were happy with everything—the cheapest accommodations, the old buses, the more than modest food. We made it through the Iron Curtain, and nobody could keep us inside anymore. The moment I would board a bus to go on a trip, all the fears of a stateless emigrant were gone, and I was my former self. The ecstasy of seeing the world was so sharp that all these years I have strived to keep it this way, not to lose this joy of seeing and experiencing something for the first time.

There were no tours to Milan, but the trains in Italy were very inexpensive. Boris and I bought the cheapest tickets and went to Milan—the night on a train, the day in Milan, and the night on a train. We were tired, but we saw the Duomo (the beautiful Milan Cathedral) and *The Last Supper* by Leonardo da Vinci. Milan during the Christmas season was extremely impressive. Illuminated streets, old signoras in long mink coats, elegant men and women; it was like a scene from the Italian movies we loved so much.

It is hard to explain to a sane person how people could deny better food to their family and spend the little money they had on travel. It is something a person raised without any restrictions would have a difficult time understanding. For forty years, we knew that we would never see Italy, but here we were, and for us, it was much more than just sightseeing—it was the tangible proof that we were finally free.

CHAPTER 48

Ladispoli (continued)

In November, our Lena, a true granddaughter of my parents, met a couple of Russian-born Israelis touring Europe and brought them to our apartment. They had sleeping bags with them and happily camped on our marble floors. We spent two days with them, learning about life in Israel, finding mutual acquaintances, and having a good time. When they left and we went outside, we found a new Ladispoli. For the first time, the American consulate started dishing out refusals to enter the United States.

The mood change was noticeable. Little by little, we learned more. The new refuseniks were all highly educated people—PhDs, medical doctors, engineers. To explain this phenomenon, I can only guess that the people in the American consulate knew almost nothing about Soviet reality. They had no idea that medical doctors and engineers did not have high salaries, and that dentists were among the lowest paid people in the Soviet Union. A good education and an interesting job were more important to these people than money, most likely an unfamiliar notion to the clerks deciding their fate.

Many former Soviet citizens had an inherent disrespect for the authorities. They reacted to the news by falsifying data on their applications. The economists were becoming house cleaners on paper, the engineers were calling themselves manual laborers, and the poor doctors became butchers—all depending on the creativity of the applicants. No one would verify this anyway.

Our questionnaires were already filled in and filled in truthfully. I am ashamed to admit that we were also anxious—ashamed because, after all, Israel would have taken us. We made the decision to go to the United States after many long discussions. We knew that America had many more universities than Israel and believed that Boris would have better opportunities to do his beloved math there.

Meanwhile, the number of new refuseniks was growing. Many years later, we learned the underlying reason for it. The American administration, faced with the rising cost of resettling an unexpectedly large number of new immigrants, made a policy change. Starting in September of 1988, the Immigration and Naturalization Service (INS) no longer automatically designated Soviet Jews as refugees; they had to "demonstrate real fear of persecution in their country of origin."

I have also recently discovered in the archives of the Jewish Telegraph Agency the following explanation of the strategy of Jewish organizations: "The increasing flow of Soviet Jewish refugees into Italy is straining the budgets of Jewish relief organizations. It is also creating potential problems in the towns where they are temporarily housed awaiting visas for the United States and elsewhere. Officials of Jewish relief agencies say that in light of tightened United States immigration policy, an effort is being made to encourage the Soviet Jews to immigrate to Israel instead of to the United States."

All our lives we had a "real fear of persecution" but what kind of "legal proof" could we or other immigrants present to the authorities? The selection process was extremely subjective. There was no difference between the new refuseniks and the admittees. There were even "double refuseniks"—those who spent years as refuseniks in the Soviet Union and finally got out of the country, only to be rejected by the United States.

As usual, the sadness was intermixed with the comical. Our neighbor in Ladispoli with the last name Ivanov (an archetypal Russian name) went through three stages. First, he was very upset about the new situation. Then, after his interview at the consulate, he came back reassured. He was telling everyone that Americans knew who was persecuted and who was not. Since he, Ivanov, was a real victim of anti-Semitism, he, of course, would be granted the refugee status. Unfortunately, he soon received a refusal. Then he again became very vocal about the unfairness of the selection process.

The children on the streets of Ladispoli were playing "the interview in the consulate." Sometimes old acquaintances would try to avoid contact with their less fortunate friends because they either felt uncomfortable with them or thought that there was no smoke without fire.

Another observation, not necessarily new, from our Ladispoli time: It is very easy to find excuses for almost anything. It was by no means wartime or a concentration camp; it was just a stressful time for some and possibly even an enjoyable time for others. Still, a number of people, who probably all their lives seemed decent to their friends, completely lost their moral core.

A PhD from Leningrad managed to rent a closet to our friends. There were six people in their family, and they were looking for a two-room apartment. They met this man, who told them that he'd be happy to sublet two rooms to them.

When they came to see the apartment, they saw only one of the rooms. The PhD told them that someone is not feeling well and is currently sleeping in the next room. He gave them a detailed description of the second room and asked them to pay in advance. The price was reasonable, so they paid and left. When, several days later, they arrived with their luggage to take possession of their rooms, they realized that the so-called "second room" was actually a small closet.

The PhD, of course, did not return the money. He continued to share the apartment with them for the following two months as if nothing happened. When confronted, he offered the following explanation: "At your age, you should've been smarter." Our friends survived, of course. I would be very interested to know how this PhD person is doing now. Is he upset about the low level of morality in our society? Does he have friends? Is he trying to instill moral values in his children? Does he even remember this episode?

CHAPTER 49

The Interview

One day in November, we were finally granted an interview at the American consulate in Rome. Dressed in our Soviet best, slightly shaking in our shoes, we went to the train station. I was very aware of the inappropriateness of my clothes. I wanted to look more elegant—perhaps Italian or French or, even better, American—but had no idea how to do it and no means to do it, even if I had known how.

Irina, at that age, did not tolerate either trains or buses well. Sometimes she just complained about being sick with nothing to show for it, but this was a special day, so she projectile vomited right on me. When we arrived at the Termini train station in Rome, I washed her face and cleaned myself the best I could, but I strongly suspected that I smelled of more than just my best perfume.

Thus encouraged, we arrived at the interview. While we were waiting in the hall, an Italian employee of the consulate noticed Irina and brought her coworkers to admire the *"bella bambina,"* the beautiful baby of mine. Irina really liked the attention and smiled benevolently at her admirers, who praised her dark curly hair and blue eyes so expressively that even we were able to understand their fast Italian.

Finally, we were invited into a room where a young-looking man, most likely a consul, greeted us with his big American smile. Many of his questions were totally unexpected. He seemed mostly interested in Boris's membership in the American Mathematical Society (AMS). He asked Boris where its headquarters were, how he became an AMS member, and other similar questions. At the time, this seemed weird, but we later read those members of American societies had certain advantages where admittance to the United States was concerned.

An interesting side note: Boris's AMS membership was on our application only because of his persistence. Among the emigrants were those aiming for Australia or Canada. Their consideration took much longer, usually nine months to a year, and HIAS loved hiring them to help with some chores. These positions of power gave some of them a profound feeling of self-importance. One such man was helping people fill in the forms. We had already heard about him from a woman we knew very well. She had been a chemical engineer for many years, but this much younger man humiliated her, told her that she was lying, and tried to ask her some ridiculous questions to prove her wrong.

He did not ask us any professional questions; he just tore up the questionnaire because Boris had included the AMS in the list of all the societies where he was a member. "We are interested only in your Komsomol and Communist Party memberships," he said, and his "we" sounded extremely important. Boris would not be Boris if he did not put it back.

The consul spoke English with Boris and me, sometimes smiling at the rest of the family. He was very friendly which, as we learned at the Ladispoli fountain, meant nothing; it was in the nature of Americans to be polite. In the end, he wished us good luck.

When we left the room, I had to explain to Boris what "good luck" meant. The poll showed that we evaluated our performance differently. Boris and his parents believed that it was a disaster, but Lena and I had a good feeling which, of course, was just that—a feeling. Irina did not express any opinion; she was very tired and sleepy, and Boris had to carry her all the way to Termini. We boarded the train for Ladispoli, feeling very uncertain about the future.

...but had no idea how to do it and no means to do it,

even if I had known how.

CHAPTER 50

December

Together with the changes in the mood in Ladispoli, the weather also changed. We were told that in 1988, the month of December was unusually cold. I grew up in cold Belarus, and now live in cold Michigan, but for a very long time, in my memory, Italy was the coldest place in the world. It was not a good combination—the marble floors, the cold wind and dampness from the sea nearby, and no money to heat our apartment. The apartment was equipped with electric heaters, and we had to feed them money. When we tried to use them, our liras disappeared with unbelievable speed.

We usually fed the heaters only when we were giving Irina a bath, which was not a simple chore. In Vienna, she got scared by a noisy bathroom fan, and since then, where the bath was concerned, our cute little angel was turning into a real warrior. We talked, we begged. I made up stories about the joys of being clean. We tried to bribe her. Nothing worked. The only way was to use brutal force. Typically, three people held her while I gave her a bath. After that, we were all wet, but I was always relieved that the neighbors did not call the police on us, since Irina was screaming bloody murder the whole time. These were also the only moments in December when I was warm, even hot from the great effort.

The decision came in mid-December. America granted us refugee status. Our departure to the United States was scheduled for December 29. We asked them to send us to Stamford, Connecticut, where our close friends—the Landreses—lived, and they granted our wish. Boris and I went to Rome and celebrated by buying a small bag of roasted chestnuts for *mille lire* (one thousand liras), approximately one dollar at that time. The chestnuts tasted wonderful. It was a combined taste of winter, of Italy, of freedom, of our new life.

The joy of this day was intermixed with sadness. Our friends, who emigrated the day before us and were as much refugees as we were, were denied entry. We went to visit them almost every day and felt extremely uncomfortable with this unfairness. When we came to the United States, one of our first priorities was to help them. We mobilized all our friends to write letters to their senators. I even went to the town hall meeting with Connecticut's then Senator-elect Joe Lieberman, who promised to help. Lena organized her high school class to write a letter in their defense. Our friends came to the United States several months after us, a little earlier than many other refuseniks.

The last week in Italy is a bit blurry. I got virulently sick with the flu and spent all of it in our cold room with a very high fever. Lena and I tenderly called this room a punishment cell; we could see our breath there. Lena, always a trooper, packed all of our eight suitcases. On December 29, 1988, we said goodbye to Ladispoli. Pan Am's Rome-New York flight took us to what was to become our new home.

CHAPTER 51

Arrival

Our arrival (photo by A. Makovoz)

On December 29, 1988, our family arrived at JFK International Airport. Here we are, stepping into our new country, and into the arms of our friends who met us at the door.

I can see my in-laws in their mid-sixties, exhausted from the flight. My father-in-law looks lost in the huge bedlam that JFK was (and still is). Boris is, as usual, full of energy and vigor; his optimism and curiosity are obvious to any viewer. Since we had no money, I was cutting the hair of all family members, including myself. I am very relieved to see that Boris's hair actually looks good. I am as skinny as a toothpick. I see sixteen-year-old Lena, a little scared, a little shy, but full of hope. Irina is three, with round cheeks and lots of curly hair. She is sleepy and tired. HIAS got us tickets in the smoking section of the plane, and all the way, she was coughing, complaining about her ears, wanting to go home—the familiar routine. None of us slept much on this flight.

I don't need this photo to remind me of what I felt—I will never forget it. Like most immigrants in United States history, we were penniless, scared, but very determined to make it work. This moment was the end of one journey and the beginning of another, which I hoped would be long and happy.

Two years before this day, I wrote a poem. The poem was about a crossing I would make one day, leaving one shore and reaching another. I wrote in it that on this new shore I'll grow taller and younger. I wrote that God would answer my prayers and grant happiness to my children. I promised to build a palace with a crystal roof there. I also wrote about my love for people on the other shore, the shore I just left. Strangely enough, this poem, written long before actual immigration, was a summary of my feelings at that moment: I hoped for the best. I was sad. I was hopeful. I had reached another shore. I was beginning a new chapter in my life, but the old one was not finished yet, not as long as I had so many people dear to me on the other shore—the shore that I left forever.

*We are finally Americans
(February 1989)*

Now, looking back, I cannot call this poem prophetic. In my new life, I did not become younger. I did become taller, though, at least in some sense, because here I found the respect and the equality that I was never able to find in my birth country.

Our new journey was not always easy. We were stateless for six years, had never before seen an ATM or a copy machine, had no idea how to write a check, and made many funny mistakes. We borrowed money and later paid every penny back. We bought our first car for 500 dollars. Good people helped us write our résumés.

I am still asking God to protect my children, my family. I didn't build a palace, but we built a house, and though its roof is not made from crystal, both our children and we ourselves call it home. Many years after the day I am describing in this chapter, I can honestly say that I have arrived. This country was very kind to our family, and we always celebrate this day. God bless America; it needs that now more than ever.

Like most immigrants in United States history, we were penniless, scared, *but very determined to make it work.*

Afterword

Professor Mordukhovich

After thirty-five years in the United States, I can summarize what happened to us in our second life.

Speaking of a brain drain, Boris's director was right. Boris is a very successful and well-respected mathematician. He became a tenured full professor from the very beginning. He is now a distinguished professor and the author of over five hundred highly cited papers and many monographs. He advised more than thirty PhD students and most of them are now professors themselves. Boris has multiple doctor honoris causa degrees. He is in high demand, travels extensively, and has visited more than one hundred countries.

I, who was unable to find a satisfying job in my native country, had a successful career in computer science, working first for private software companies and then for the University of Michigan. I never failed an interview, always got at least three offers, and, most importantly, enjoyed my challenging job and was well-respected and, I hope, liked by my colleagues. I am still friends with many of them. I am not writing it to brag; I just want to show the difference between two countries.

I enjoy wildlife photography, have published a children's book, and write a travel blog.

Together with Boris, I traveled the world. We visited all seven continents, saw all five oceans, and crossed the equator multiple times, both by air and by sea. We saw places I never thought I would see and did things I never thought I would do. We visited Antarctica and the Arctic Circle. We sailed the Amazon River and the Yangtze, climbed volcanoes, stepped on the deep ocean floor, visited Buddhist temples and Islamic mosques, climbed Mayan and Aztec temples, saw *moai* statues on Easter Island and the Taj Mahal in India. We enjoyed Petra and Patagonia,

Some of our adventures

visited Tierra del Fuego and Ayers Rock, the Galápagos Islands and Spitsbergen. We snorkeled in the Great Barrier Reef and swam in the Dead Sea, rode elephants and camels, hugged koalas, and fed llamas.

I was robbed at knifepoint in Guatemala, visited dangerous sights in Rio de Janeiro, almost froze while photographing penguins, became seasick in the Drake Passage, and nearly fainted from heat at Angkor Wat. I flew to Japan with a herniated disk and developed asthma in China. I regret many things but never my crazy adventures, and I will always be grateful to my new country for allowing me to experience them and to see the world.

Lena

Lena came to the United States several months short of seventeen. She did not have it easy. It took her a while to find friends. In half a year, she had to learn English well enough to pass the SAT with a good score. She managed to do it and was admitted to the very prestigious University of Michigan. She earned both her bachelor of science and master of science degrees there and became a computer scientist. Lena has built a very successful career. She raised three beautiful daughters while creating and running a flourishing business.

Since the events of October 7, 2023, in Israel, Lena has been making me more and more proud every day. In her big city, she became a leader in the fight against the anti-Semitism, uniting the people with different backgrounds and political affiliations in this noble mission.

Our Irina grew up in America. After getting her bachelor of science degree from the University of Michigan, she left Ann Arbor and received her master of science degree and PhD in epidemiology. She was

Irina

a postdoc at Harvard and stayed there to work on research. She has published many papers and conducted a very famous study on flight attendants. We were very proud to hear her name on TV and read it in multiple newspapers. She combines her brilliant career with raising three children.

My children are my pride and joy. They are honest, kind, hardworking, and spiritual. They are the best thing that ever happened to me, and I love them with all my heart.

All six grandchildren

It is impossible to get our grandchildren together for a nice photo. The latest picture of all six I have is from six years ago.

They are growing fast. Becky got her bachelor's degree and is preparing now for LSAT, the Law School Admission Test. Polly is a university student now. Little Mia is not that little anymore. The baby in this photo, Natan, our youngest, is already six. Aron is twelve, and Yael is nine. Each of the cousins is unique; they have very different personalities and different talents, and it makes watching them grow extremely interesting. Three of our grandchildren know Russian very well; the three youngest know two Russian words: *babushka* and *dedushka*, which mean grandma and grandpa. I love them all, and I wish each of them all the happiness in the world.

When we came to this country, I thought that we solved at least one problem. Our children and grandchildren will never have to face anti-Semitism. The events of October 7, 2023, showed how wrong I was. Painfully familiar to us, anti-Zionism again marches in lockstep with anti-Semitism, only now it happens in America. I still believe that this country will overcome it, but my grandchildren should be prepared to educate, to stand for what they believe in, and to fight if needed. I hope they will never be ashamed of their roots and their identity.

I would be remiss if I did not mention our two dogs.

This is our beautiful poodle, Wuffy, the craziest but most devoted dog in the world.

Wuffy the Wonder Dog

He ate half of our house, destroyed pieces of furniture and windowsills, preferred the taste of Russian books to that of English ones, could open any door, and was smarter than both of us combined

Ten minutes before I came home from work, he would always wait for me at the door, enthusiastically wagging his tail. When I was sick, he never left my side. The moment I felt better, he would go on one of his adventures. I will always remember him running to me, his ears flapping in the air, and all the love and devotion in his big eyes.

When we brought Lovie home, he was eight weeks old and the size of a small kitten. I guess after Wuffy we deserved a mellow dog, and Lovie was the easiest dog one can imagine. He was funny and intuitive, intelligent and loyal.

He was adored by our grandchildren and loved by our friends. When Boris left home for a business trip, he would spend two minutes saying goodbye to me and five to Lovie.

Lovie

The last few years were tough for both him and us. Lovie was a cancer survivor and diabetic. I drove him for two hours one-way for his cancer surgery and then for chemotherapy. I gave him insulin shots twice a day. He was blind, but he always found my hand to lick it. I miss him dearly.

I got more love than I deserve from my dogs. I am sure that when I cross the bridge, both of them will run to me with their ears flapping and their tails wagging at unbelievable speed.

I have not had an easy life. I had more than my share of illnesses and accidents, of discrimination and hardships, of difficult people near me, and of obstacles that I had to overcome. Still, I consider myself lucky. I love my family and my friends, nature and poetry, books and music, spring and fall, birds and animals. I worked hard, and I was always trying to do my best. I love my country; I look forward to new adventures, to happy family events, meetings with friends, and quiet evenings with books. And no matter how I feel, I look at myself in the mirror in the morning and I smile.

And I smile...

The End!

Acknowledgments

I am extremely grateful to:

My editor, Michael Savikovsky, for making this book so much better.

Tatyana Barochin, Galina Savikovsky, and Greg Kosinovsky for their precious feedback on this book.

My close friends the Landreses and the Savikovskys for their enthusiastic support and encouragement when I really needed it.

My family and friends for their valuable contribution to this book.

My daughter Lena Kosinovsky for being my pillar of strength and for making it all happen.

Boris for motivating me and for always believing in me.

About the Author

Margaret Mordukhovich was born in the former Soviet Union. She comes from a long line of rabbis and Talmudic scholars, and the authorities disenfranchised many members of her family due to suppression of religion and rampant antisemitism. Her early childhood memories were filled with horrors of the Stalin era and stories about the Second World War and the Holocaust. This background taught Margaret to think independently, even in the face of massive Soviet propaganda.

Her parents always encouraged Margaret's passion for reading. Although the family did not have much money, there were always a lot of books in their home.

Margaret has been thinking up stories and writing poems since before she can remember. Her early verses were printed in children's newspapers. At sixteen, she appeared on local radio and TV in her native city of Minsk to present her poetry, resulting in a long-running daily load of fan mail. Later, she fell in love with mathematics, in which she earned a Master of Science degree.

Margaret came to the United States as a political refugee with her husband and two daughters. Upon leaving the Soviet Union, virtually all they could take with them was their education. It was a very difficult transition, but one she is proud to have experienced. This country became home for her and her family.

Margaret had a successful career as a Computer Scientist and has lived in Ann Arbor, Michigan, for more than 35 years. She enjoys traveling, wildlife photography, reading, and, writing.

Fully bilingual and shaped by two great cultures, American and Russian, Margaret writes a Russian-language travel blog and has published a children's book, *Wuffy the Wonder Dog*, in English.

Order books

via Amazon.com

Order books in bulk via
books.myfirstlife@gmail.com

Connect

my-first-life.com

Read Margaret's travel blog in Russian:
maratravelblog.com

www.ingramcontent.com/pod-product-compliance
Lightning Source LLC
Chambersburg PA
CBHW020227130626
46549CB00005B/1779